Wisdom Keys for Moving Forward in Life and Love After Death Do Us Part

AN ANTHOLOGY

Praise for

A Widow's Resilience

"Single, married, divorced, engaged, married again, widowed. After 17 years, and just when I was ready to finish out my life alone, God sent me His best. If you desire to move forward in life and love, allow the living experiences shared within the pages of 'A Widow's Resilience' to encourage you. I'm 79 years old and will be married again soon. I'm happier than I've ever been. God is looking at YOUR husband – right now!"

—Dr. Mary Darlene Edwards
Founder, Widow's With Wisdom
Author, *Transition: From Widowhood to Womanhood*

"As a mental health professional, I have worked for years helping people effectively handle loss. This anthology is a roadmap for women who walk this path of loss and living/loving beyond it. I recommend these stories which will inspire, impact, inform, and invigorate you at your core. This work teaches that just because you have loved and lost, does not mean you are not loving, loveable, nor that you will not love again.....Thank you ladies for allowing your journeys to teach others!"

—Dr. Sabrina Jackson, "The People Expert"
Founder, Essential Colors

"'*A Widow's Resilience: Wisdom Keys for Moving Forward in Life and Love After Death Do Us Part'* is a powerfully inspiring book that will undoubtedly reach the masses with intimate experiences that speak to the heart of women who have experienced loss, pain or even grief. The personal testimonies shared in *'A Widow's Resilience'* provide a deep oasis of hope, with the intention to move the reader forward in life. All who read it will be moved, inspired, and encouraged to keep living, growing, creating, and loving again."

—Dr. Charisse Staine
Pastor, Detroit Worship Center
-excerpted from the Foreword

"As a Pastor, Christian Counselor and once a widow myself, I am confident that these powerful and very personal life stories of love, saying goodbye to a beloved husband, and learning to live again here in the pages of 'A Widow's Resilience' will be tools to bring healing to grieving hearts. Situations and circumstances may be different, but the heart of God is the same towards us, His daughters: He is faithful and He cares for us. This absolute truth shines through in each of these testimonies. If you are a widow, grieving, alone, scared, angry, abandoned, uncertain, feeling life is surreal or that you can't go on, read this book! Let these stories minister to your heart that God has a future for you that is filled with joy and success, just like these women."

—Cheryl Ward, Pastor
Word of Faith International Christian Centre
Toronto, Ontario

"The stories penned in this book are from women who understand God's amazing grace, His supernatural strength, and a peace that surpasses the unimaginable. Having personally walked through widowhood, I understand the depths of such a great loss. I pray that you draw from their courage, be enlightened by their journey, and glean from their strength."

—Kim McQuitty, Author/Speaker
Founder, Wife Ready

"I want to congratulate LaTanya Orr and her 13 writers for this much needed book, 'A Widow's Resilience.' I became a widow at 35 years old. The death of a spouse places the widow in a new situation; however, it is important to know that you can begin again; there is life after death. I understand the importance of needing someone to be transparent with you through this major transition. This book is written to help you through your transformation; for new purposes, new interests as you embrace your new life without your spouse. I know these stories about 'Resilience' will bring you hope, comfort, healing and the ability to 'bounce back'."

—Miranda Fay Pope, Pastor
Rapha Ministries International

TRANSFORMATIONAL STORIES OF TRAGEDY TO TRIUMPH

RESILIENCE

Wisdom Keys for Moving Forward in Life and Love After Death Do Us Part

AN ANTHOLOGY

Compiled by

LaTANYA ORR RICHARD

A Widow's Resilience: Wisdom Keys for Moving Forward in Life and Love After Death Do Us Part
First edition - Volume 1: June 2021
ISBN: 978-0-578-85280-5

For permission requests, contact hello@awidowsresilience.com.

Purchases can be made at www.awidowsresilience.com
hello@awidowsresilience.com

Unless otherwise indicated, all Scripture quotations marked (KJV) are from the King James YouVersion Bible App 2021.

The events and conversations in this book have been set down to the best of the author's ability, although some names and details have been changed to protect the privacy of individuals. Any resemblance to persons living or dead should be plainly apparent to them and those who know them, especially if the author has been kind enough to have provided their real names. All events described herein actually happened, though on occasion the author has taken certain, very small, liberties with chronology, because that is their rights as Americans.

CREDITS

Publishing services provided by Selah Branding & Design LLC
LaTanya Orr, Producer/Curator
www.iselah.com

Editor: @ê˙] onica Handy

Inside Layout/Typesetting Design: Candice Holt, World Media House LLC

Cover Design: LaTanya Orr

Supporting Design: Harry Lawson

For information about speaking engagements, special discounts for bulk purchases or other inquiries, please contact LaTanya Orr at hello@awidowsresilience.com

Printed in the United States of America.

DEDICATION

This project is dedicated to every woman whose heart has been broken by the loss of a husband. May these stories serve as a source of hope and resilience for cherishing the memories while celebrating your new season of living God's purpose for your life.

FOREWORD

The glory of this latter house shall be greater than of the former, saith the LORD of hosts: and in this place will I give peace, saith the LORD of hosts. – Haggai 2:9

A Widow's Resilience: Wisdom Keys in Moving Forward in Life and Love After Death Do Us Part is a powerfully inspiring book that will rouse the masses with intimate experiences that speak to the heart of women who have endured loss, pain, and grief. The personal testimonies provide a deep oasis of hope, with the intention of moving the reader forward in life. Oftentimes, women who suffer the passing of a spouse find themselves in positions of: confusion, anger, frustration, depression, shame, embarrassment, paralyzing fear, and anxiety leading to stagnation. When the role of wife has expired, women are frequently left trying to either reinvent, recreate, or realize who they will become and how they will live without their spouse.

Like Movement Founder, LaTanya Orr, the compassion that I have for widows is not unfounded. One weekday morning, my husband left for an annual conference that we normally would attend together. Four days later, he was gone. Clinging to every scripture that I knew, I professed the Word of God and stood in faith, until I was forced to embrace my new future without my husband of 25 years.

With three young adult children and one adolescent, I never thought that I would be a widow at 47 years old. Nothing will prepare you to experience the death of a spouse, especially a sudden and unexpected death.

While mourning is a natural part of the process, I determined that I would not stay in that place indefinitely. Mourning would not consume my life, I had to live. Haggai 2:9 was my mantra and I confessed within my heart, despite what I had experienced in loss, that my latter would be greater than the former. No matter how great the past was, my future had to be greater. This was not a slight on what was, but a spotlight on what I expected. I chose to take a future-oriented perspective on my destiny. As I worked through this process, I chose to move forward, and only forward, period! Forward meant devoting myself to my children, the ministry, entrepreneurial endeavors, and work. I remained focused on these things while emerging with a mindset that I did not want to ever marry again. Therefore, I did not date nor entertain any opportunities to date.

Nearly two years into widowhood, God had a different plan. After receiving a call that my uncle was in ICU and did not have much time to live, I drove to the state where he was hospitalized. I needed to be there to pray for him and accompany my mother, who would also be arriving. During this process, God reconnected me with my college sweetheart from nearly 30 years prior. We had never seen nor talked to each other in all that time. He was my best friend in college, my protector, and my college love. When we connected, it was as if we never parted.

Four months later, I abandoned widowhood for marriage to the only person who I would ever consider marrying. I regained my former best friend, protector, and love again.

I want to thank Mrs. LaTanya Orr Richard for the opportunity to write the foreword to this wonderful book. Her thoughtful and compassionate heart and widowhood experience would not let her neglect the need to share messages of hope and healing for those in whose place she once stood. I pray that all who read it will be moved, inspired, and encouraged to keep living, growing, creating, and loving again.

Forward in Life and Love,

Charisse M. Staine M.A., M.Ed., LLPC, NCC, ND
Pastor. Psychologist. Professional Counselor. Naturopath.

About Chaisse M. Staine, M.A., M.Ed., LLPC, NCC, ND

Dr. Charisse M. Staine has 30 years of experience teaching, motivating, and mentoring individuals to live their best lives - spirit, soul, and body. She esteems each individual as a multi-faceted person capable of great exploits and has devoted her life to helping others. Her approach to life is joyful, future oriented, and resilient. Over the years, she has been known as a Wife, Mother, Influential Pastor/Teacher, Author, Chef, Board Certified Naturopath, Integrative Nutrition Coach, Professional Counselor, and former Michigan State Champion Powerlifter.

Dr. Charisse is currently the Pastor/Founder of Detroit Worship Center and Founder/CEO of The Center for Peak Performance. You can find her on Instagram @peakperformancegroups and @drcharisse

ACKNOWLEDGMENTS

First, I must give honor to God who is head of my life for His divine wisdom, favor, and inspiration to produce this special work.

As curator and producer of this project, I am indebted to Monica Handy for her godly-inspired editorial skills to the stories within these pages. For this book, she provided her gifted "handiwork" with intention and grace. I am also grateful for my extraordinary design team of Harry Lawson and Candice Holt. Appreciate your creative ingenuity. Bravo!

Thanks to those who encouraged, interviewed, moderated our ClubHouse chats or supported in other capacities along the way — Dr. Lisa Wicker, Kim McQuitty, Pastor Cheryl Ward, Dr. Charisse Gibert Staine, Dr. Sabrina Jackson, Dr. Mary Edwards, Pastor Miranda Fay Pope, Caryl Lucas, Espy "Ettafly" Thomas, Raquelle "Rocki" Harris, Lendell McEwen, Dr. Eugenia Orr, Megan Kirk, Monica Hickson, Leslie Morris, Sherrell Straker-Valdezloqui, Denitra Townsend Gregory, Tisha Hammond, Charlene Mitchell-Rodgers, my admin assistant Angela Williamson and to my husband, Melvin Richard.

Lastly, a very special thanks to the co-authors of this project. Without your commitment and transparency, this book just would not be. May God add a 100-fold blessing to each of you for your patience throughout the publishing process. Ladies, it's AWRAP!

TABLE OF CONTENT

Introduction

p. xv

Leslie Graham Andrews

From Hell to Happiness-The Steps to Take on Your Journey Back to Joy

p. 23

Marlo Beamon

All Is Well

p. 34

Patrice Caldwell Gabriel

Boomerang

p.46

Veronica Corbett West

A Widow's Peak

p. 57

Kiko Davis Snoddy

Soulful Mourning

p. 67

Barbra Gentry-Pugh

When Life Stopped, When Life Began

p. 85

Linda Hannah
To Love and Love Again
p. 98

Doris Hannah Turner
Brighter Days Ahead
p. 113

LaCharmine (L.A.) Jefferson
Honor Him and him by Living Your Life
p. 129

Grace Liang
Gracefully Grieving
p. 146

Monica Morgan
True Love Never Dies
p. 156

Wilma Parham
Changeless Love
p. 172

Beatrice Yesufu
A Renewed Mind of a Warrior Widow
p. 187

Afterword
p. 200

*Is there no balm in Gilead; is there no physician there?
Why then is not the health of the daughter of
my people recovered?*

Jeremiah 8:22 (KJV)

INTRODUCTION

From my experience, I have discovered that grief is never easy nor polite; it doesn't show up at your convenience with social grace, manners, or respect. Nevertheless, its presence cannot be avoided by the affected party or judged by onlookers. It is, in fact, a unique journey molded by the individual experience.

But, what if I told you there was a way to make the unsure places in grieving bearable? What if I shared the pathways of survivors who overcame grief and learned to live and love again? Would you then dare to believe that there is light beyond the shadows?

The purpose of this book is to show you that you are not alone. There is indeed an entire community of women willing to be transparent about their tragedies and gripping grief that should have robbed them of their Jeremiah 29:11 future. Instead of recoiling, they chose to rise as a collective force of wisdom keyholders entitled: "*A Widows Resilience.*"

I chose the word "resilience" because it is a term that directs one's gaze forward, bears weight, and signifies the capacity to rise.

Merriam Webster defines "resilient" as:

a: capable of withstanding shock without permanent deformation or rupture.

b: tending to recover from or adjust easily to misfortune or change.

1. *Springing back; rebounding.*
2. *Returning to the original form or position after being bent, compressed, or stretched.*
3. *Recovering readily from illness, depression, adversity, or the like; buoyant.*
   - MerriamWebster.com

Resilience is that ineffable quality that allows some people to be knocked down by life and come back stronger than ever. Rather than letting failure or grief overcome you and drain your resolve, you find a way to rise from the ashes. Psychologists have identified factors that make someone resilient, among them — a positive attitude, optimism, the ability to regulate emotions, and the ability to see failure as a form of helpful feedback. Even after misfortune, resilient people are blessed with such a positive outlook empowering them to change course and soldier on.

In the forthcoming chapters, discover how these stories cultivate an open forum about rarely touched issues. Equally important is their capacity to arouse, encourage, and incite the release of keys that unlock stagnation, prompt prayer, and offer a new frame of reference. Transformation is then sure to follow.

I'll begin this journey by sharing — that, like countless women in my position — my husband and I had plans. Even as recent as three weeks before my beloved husband passed, we talked about going to Catalina Island off the coast of California. His return home from rehab would mark the arrival of Spring. He said, "I only need two to three more weeks in rehab, and I'll be home. Then we'll go on a much-needed vacation."

When I say that I didn't see his death coming — that would be an understatement. As an entrepreneur for nearly 20 years, I was juggling my most hectic work season with visiting my husband at the hospital EVERY DAY! Everything was due at the same time. We had been — what we both thought — through the worst of the illness a month before. Twenty-one days in rehab, doing great, then the unthinkable happened. My husband's health spiraled out of control.

In 72 hours, my Jimmie went from laughing and singing to not being able to talk. Really? It was like a scene from the movie "The Matrix." Everything seemed to be happening in slow motion, but yet, fast-forward, out of the doctors' and my husband's control. But God.

Out of his own mouth, he had declared that he was a walking, talking miracle- more than a conqueror- he was going to walk out of the hospital. "All is well"...he said..."I love you, baby."

I replayed our last conversations over and over in my mind — hoping to hear something different — than the always affirming, never complaining words he spoke to me those last few days he was able to speak.

We had plans... His 49th birthday party plans... Travel plans to the ocean - anywhere there was a beach. Bike rides on Belle Isle. Dancing. Relaxing while sipping a cool drink on the front porch of our new home. Visiting my mother and sister in Chicago. Completing his book. Getting a puppy. So much we were going to do together and separately. To say the very least, we had plans.

'For I know the plans and thoughts that I have for you,' says the LORD, 'plans for peace and well-being and not for disaster to give you a future and a hope.'

- Jeremiah 29:11

In her book "Life Interrupted," author and minister Priscilla Shirer admonishes...

"Back away from the immediate shock... Begin to see every interruption as a divine intervention... It may seem impossible, but God has singled-out and pin-pointed you as His partner in this particular project ...It may seem unbearable to endure, but you've been called to be the one to display His Glory. Even in your weakness and brokenness, God has purposefully given you the high honor

of being deemed suited for a task with heavenly implications. A divine partnership that will yield magnificent results for you and His kingdom... We always succeed when we surrender."

As I worked through my grief, I arrived at three wisdom keys certain to push you through the sadness and despair so you can move forward:

1. **SURRENDER** - While it may seem impossible, release, relinquish the pain and sadness. Perhaps slowly, a little bit at a time, let go and allow time to heal your heart. Lay down every emotion at the altar and don't pick it back up. Remember the good times. Hold onto the beautiful memories that you shared with your loved one. Know they would want you to live on.

2. **PRAY** - Meditate, spend time in the presence of God and His Word; immerse yourself in Scripture and grief recovery resources. Seek counsel and grief therapy. Go to God in prayer. Thank Him despite all. Confess your deepest darkest emotions. Through prayer, ask for comfort and guidance on how to move forward.

3. **NOURISH** - You must self-care. Do take time off from work/your career— perhaps put some things on hold so you can decompress and refresh. Spend quality time with your children. Start a work-out regimen to realign your body, soul, and spirit. Go to the spa or create your own in-home spa experience. If possible, take that over-due vacation or just make time for rest and relaxation. Facetime/ oom connect with loved ones for support. Even with social distancing, stay in touch with others as

much as possible. Allow yourself time to heal. These are steps to anchor your resilience — steps with which you must purposefully walk through to get through. With God's help, time will ease the pain—the emptiness, the hurt, the anxiety, feelings of uncertainty on what to do next. Seek closure and peace for those thoughts of where did I/we go wrong. Cope with the shattered dreams and plans that you had hoped for.

As I reflect on our beautiful love season, I count it all joy! I now share with other grieving women that there IS life after death do us part.

Our plans together may have been altered, but God's merciful master plan is still in effect. He is a God of Peace. Nothing missing, nothing broken. Nothing is lost in Christ. In the words of my late husband — praise God, that's what's up!

So, if you've experienced a life-altering event, grieving the death of a loved one—while it may not seem like it at the present moment, your future is bright. Beyond these pages, it is my hope that these stories coupled with God's unfailing love and your most cherished memories, will light the way forward. Indeed, all IS well.

"Disappointment is a place we pass thru,
not a place we stay."

Christine Caine
Founder, Propel Women

Side note: A year after my Jimmie departed this life, God blessed me with a new husband — Melvin. God's plans are exceedingly abundantly more than you could ever ask or think. Your story is still being told. Be open and expect to receive great things for your life even when it seems impossible.

- LaTanya Orr Richard

FROM HELL TO HAPPINESS –

The Steps To Take On Your Journey Back To Joy

BY LESLIE GRAHAM ANDREWS

Make your healing a priority and set boundaries during the grieving process.

Even though we may seek, desire, and pursue it, feeling happy is not a choice we make. Joy, on the other hand, is a choice purposefully made. It is possible to feel joy in difficult times. Joy doesn't require a smile to identify its existence, although it does feel better in the long run.

-Compassion.com

Hospital floors are hard and cold. I vividly recall the floors' hardness because my feet were killing me after walking them for 22 straight days while standing guard over my husband, Alton. He was battling a pulmonary embolism in the intensive care unit during his final hospital stay in 2010. However, I did not discover how cold the floors were until my face hit the smooth, hard surface, and I lay there, paralyzed from shock and grief. It felt like a dream sequence on some television show as doctors exited his room and walked toward me- This, of course, after working feverishly to save his life.

I was present in his room when he coded (technically died), but I was not prepared for my 6'3" lion of a husband to not survive. As they approached, all I recall hearing is, "We are sorry, Mrs. Andrews, we did all we could." Then my face was greeted by the linoleum. I was spent- The news literally knocked me off my feet, and my legs refused my command to stand. I didn't even have the energy to pull myself up into a chair, so I laid there helpless and heartbroken. Between screaming, crying, and bouts of exhaustion, I found myself the new inductee of a club whose membership no woman wants- I was now a widow. It would be days, weeks, and months later when I began to understand how this new title would transform me, my journey, and how I would experience life.

On March 15, 2010, at 9:12 a.m., my journey of love, joy, and happiness came to an end, but a new journey began at that exact moment. The lessons learned on this new journey are what I want to share to comfort, encourage, and assure you that love, and loss can exist peacefully in your heart.

Following are the five "STEPS" that brought me back from the devastation of losing the love of my life and set me firmly on the path to regaining my joy.

Full disclosure: I curse when I talk and when I write, not because I do not know other words to use, but because I choose the words that reflect my pain and passion. Apologies if this offends anyone.

Ok, hold my hand, and here we go.

***Sit in your pain, do not run from it. If you hide it, you cannot heal it.**

That's right sit in it; feel it- curse it- scream, little girl; cry, throw your body on the floor! Your heart has been ripped out of your chest, and your brain is numb; you get to express your pain any damn way you please! Express every emotion you are feeling exactly when you are feeling them, no apologies. If it makes those around you uncomfortable, refuse to give a shit! If your love felt like mine, it was the most beautiful experience ever, and the loss cut me down to my core. I am tearing up just typing about it, and it has been ten years since my husband died.

The first lesson of widowhood is that there is only one rule – be true to yourself. If you are angry, express the anger. Death is experienced like a light switch, one minute it is on, and the next minute it is turned off; gone. Just the blink of an eye and you were not ready. The gut-wrenching pain in your heart confirms as much. Even if you are blessed to be at the bedside to "say" goodbye, you are still not ready to "feel" ok with "goodbye." I can promise you this, the initial shock will wear off with time and even be manageable, but only if you choose acceptance over avoidance.

***Take all the time you need.**

Being a widow is a new role that you will learn how to perform, not perfect. One of the things you learn early on as a widow is that people are prone to say stupid shit. I mean stupid, uninformed, unproven, and unnecessary shit. In the six hours that I stood at my husband's casket during his wake, I must have heard 100 idiotic declarations about God's will, what I should do, and selfish attempts masked to relate to me but making my experience about themselves.

One insensitive comment is as follows:

"I know how you feel because when I lost my blah blah blah..."

The dumbest of them all, however, was this statement from some woman I didn't know – "You are young; there is another man out there for you. After a year or so, you will fall in love again".

Yes, someone had the unmitigated gall to say this to me standing at my husband's casket! Wait, how did I respond, you ask?

Well, at that moment of fresh grief, all of Detroit's west side was welling up and about to come out of me, but by God's grace, that crazy person was escorted out of my presence before I cut the fool up in there!

Upon reflection, there was some truth to what she said, even if her timing and delivery sucked! I was young, forty-two years old, and even if I could not fathom it then, I would love again. The only stupid part I still disagree with is it taking a year to find love. The truth that I offer you today is this - you will love again when your heart is able- when things feel different. Whenever it happens is perfectly ok. Hear me, my sister, there is no "right or wrong way to be a widow. No book of rules will or should have been mailed to you after the funeral. You are free to heal on your terms, in your own time, in your own way. Your vows said, "until death do you part," not "until the appropriate amount of time has passed."

***Establish and enforce boundaries around you and your family.**

Allow me to honor you with some hard truth – While you are grieving, there may be people around you who are plotting and planning, and it is usually your family or his friends! Someone will want some of his possessions, to borrow some insurance money they are certain you received, or hell even move in with you – to help with the kids of course!

My sister, if at all humanly possible, do not allow this to happen or you WILL regret it! Remember, no good deed goes unpunished. One request for clothing turns into an inquiry about jewelry, which leads to a call about investing in some grand scheme and ends up a discussion about money being owed. Take my experienced advice – if it is not in the will, it does not go out the door! I do not have to convince you with tales of conniving relatives and ungrateful children; we all have them in our midst. What is critical to remember is that the time wasted managing things and making other people happy delays your healing and is too expensive a price to pay for peace.

***Prioritize your healing every day, all day for as many days as it takes, period—hard stop.**

Experiencing the death of your spouse is a trauma that best responds to an extraordinary, non-negotiable level of self-care. The most important person to you right now is you. Let me say that again another way – you need to commit to being your own hero in this story.

You must preserve yourself to be there for everyone who will now look to you for everything.

There are several effective investments you can make in your healing:

Invest in a journal and a beautiful writing instrument. It would help if you made documenting your journey an intentional experience. I light my favorite fragranced candle, prepare alcohol, and allow my feelings to come pouring out onto the pages. I write until I have made peace with that day.

Place encouraging affirmations throughout your environment. Words have power, so use them to remind you, lift you and see you through the difficult moments that are guaranteed to come.

Move your body. Run, walk, cycle, practice yoga – anything that gets your blood flowing and oxygen levels up. Exercise relieves stress, anxiety and boosts your mood.

Practice meditation. There are numerous mental health benefits that you will enjoy with regular meditation: lowered blood pressure, reduced symptoms of depression, better focus and concentration are just a few.

Sleep. The one thing you will find challenging is the very thing you need to do to remain healthy enough to do anything else. Sleep deprivation is more detrimental than you could imagine. Lack of adequate sleep weakens your immune system, elevates your blood pressure, overexerts your heart, and negatively impacts your mood.

Love notes: Sis, be careful about how and when you self-medicate. Through the thick haze of grief, an occasional glass of wine can quickly evolve into a bottle of liquor; one pill for anxiety can become a dependency on the entire bottle, and hugs from a familiar man can lead to unplanned intimacy. If possible, have a sister friend keep an eye on you when possible. Pain is a dangerous motivator, and you are more vulnerable than you have ever been in your life right now.

***See the future with the eyes and heart of loving expectancy.**

"So how did you know that you were healed?"

As a person who speaks professionally about my journey as a widow, I am consistently asked this question. The honest answer is that you just feel healed. There is no clear indication that healing has happened – it just does. Unexpectedly it may happen one morning. You will wake up, and the weight of the sadness will be gone. The sun will shine brighter than it has in ages, and you will feel like getting up and participating in your life. Or the things that brought you to your knees in tears will one day only bring a smile on your face and joy to your heart.

There is no calendar date to mark; it takes as long as it takes. Just know, at some point, you will have the strength and courage to look at your life for what it still can become instead of through the lens of what you have lost. The flutter will noticeably return when you see a man that re-ignites your attraction. Flowers will smell lovely, food will taste amazing, and most importantly, your mirror will reflect the familiar, powerful smile of a woman that has been tested but not defeated. That woman WILL BE YOU!

Until that day comes, I have one last thing to share that will help you along the journey back to joy. I found reading extremely helpful as I sorted through all these new and unfamiliar feelings of loneliness and deep despair. What follows is what I call the "literary love kit."

"Literary Love Kit"

Books
"Why? – Trusting God When You Don't Understand."
Author – Anne Graham Lotz

"The Power of Now."
Author - Eckhart Tolle

"A Blessing in Disguise." (I found the chapter "Death and Dying" especially helpful
Author – Andrea Joy Cohen

"Widows Wear Stilettos – A Practical and Emotional Guide for The Young Widow."
Author – Carole Brody Fleet

"YOU Are a BADASS" – How to Stop Doubting Your Greatness and Start Living An Awesome Life."
Author – Jen Sincero

Websites
Top 60 Blogs for widows
https://blog.feedspot.com/widowblogs/

Scriptures
1 Timothy 5:3 – "Honor and help those widows who are truly widowed and without support".

Psalm 146:1 - "The Lord protects the strangers; he supports the fatherless and the widow."

Jeremiah 49:11 – "Leave your orphans behind I will keep them alive. And let your widows trust and confide in me.

In closing, my sister, let me leave you encouraged. I believe widows are God's warriors of love. He selected us to be His example of honor, commitment, and fidelity. Your grief is not in vain. It is a lived and living experience, expanding, and maturing your capacity to give and receive love. And when it is all over, it is real love that will prevail forevermore. I will leave you with God's Word to comfort you on the journey ahead. God bless you.

1 Thessalonians 4:13-18 -

"Brothers and sisters, we do not want you to be uninformed about those who sleep in death so that you do not grieve like the rest of mankind, who have no hope. For we believe that Jesus died and rose again, and so we believe that God will bring with Jesus those who have fallen asleep in him. According to the Lord's word, we tell you that we who are still alive, who are left until the coming of the Lord, will certainly not precede those who have fallen asleep. For the Lord himself will come down from heaven, with a loud command, with the voice of the archangel and with the trumpet call of God, and the dead in Christ will rise first. After that, we who are still alive and are left will be caught up together with them in the clouds to meet the Lord in the air. And so, we will be with the Lord forever. Therefore encourage one another with these words."

About Leslie Graham Andrews

After a successful 25-year tenure in corporate America, native Detroiter, Leslie Graham Andrews, launched Daisy Ventures LLC which is the parent company for three subsidiaries: Leslie Andrews Consulting, Leslie Speaks! and the lifestyle blog, "Grown Woman Chronicles.

Leslie says, "I live to inspire women," describing herself as a gardener of dreams, sowing powerful seeds into the living soil of women with care and expectancy, watering them with love, cultivating them with truth, and celebrating each of their harvests.

An avid runner, in her spare time, Leslie travels the world, maintains self-care with physical fitness and finds the most joy when building her philanthropic legacy.

Connect with Leslie Graham Andrews at leslieygraham@gmail.com

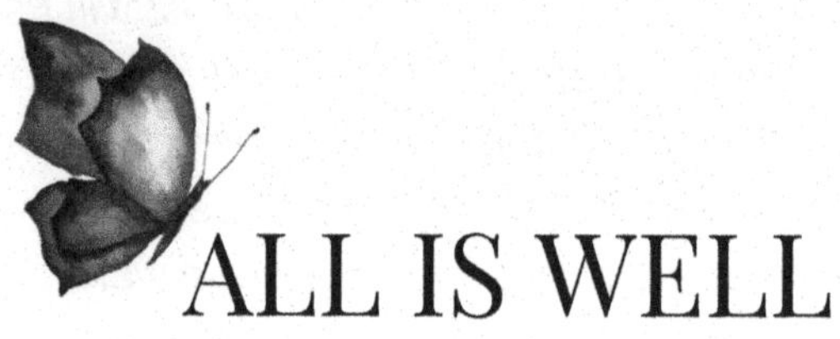

ALL IS WELL

BY MARLO BEAMON

All Is Well

My beloved husband, Kevin, and I were married for over 20 beautiful years. There was never any question about his love for me; he made absolute sure of that. When we got married in 1999, Kevin was a businessman. Over the years of serving together in ministry, we began to understand there was a higher calling on our lives. However, it would be 15 years later, when Kevin became a minister, that our calling would emerge with clarity.

I had no idea that God's vision for our lives was so grand! Because of our love for helping couples, I thought we would have a marriage ministry at our home, so when my husband told me he was ready to answer the call and launch a church, I agreed, shaking and trembling! Nevertheless by December 2017, along with our co-laborers in Christ, we launched "Word of Faith Community Church" in Acworth, Georgia. I must say that launching and establishing a church is not for the faint of heart; it is a labor of love requiring: prayer, fasting, resources, and people with a heart to serve. To have all the above, was a blessing, as well as the amazing support we received from our home church, Word of Faith Family Worship Cathedral under the leadership of our Bishop Dale C. Bronner.

Kevin, was now the Senior Pastor of our newly planted church, and was lovingly called Rev. Kev. Unexpectedly in January 2019, he had a mild heart attack that we learned was caused by atrial fibrillation. Over the next 14 months, we drew even closer together as a couple as his health declined and he had to have multiple procedures. I went to every appointment, procedure, and surgery and I was by his side every step of the way. We remained hopeful during this trial, but unbeknownst to me, the Lord was strengthening me for what was yet to come.

As I reflect over that time, I realize how Kevin shared things with me that left clues about how we would carry on in his absence as a church. We were a great team.

In March of 2020, the Holy Spirit whispered something I wasn't prepared to hear. I heard Him say, "he passed away" as the paramedics were rushing him off to the hospital. Still pressing in my faith, I sat in the hospital's waiting area between my anxiety and my armor-bearers, believing for the best. Just as I inquired of my armor-bearers "what today's date" was, the doctor came in to notify me that my husband had passed away.

Even though the doctor's words confirmed what the Holy Spirit had whispered to me earlier, I still was not prepared for what I had just heard. I was in complete shock and total disbelief! I couldn't grasp the reality of it, nor could I rationalize how this could happen after we trusted God to heal him. It just didn't make sense! How could I go on? What would I do, and where would I start? I lost my husband and best friend, and I wasn't sure how I could move on without him.

I was confused and angry with God. I found myself questioning God about how He could let this happen. I would ask, "Lord, why did you call us to launch a church and then take my husband/Pastor from me?" It just didn't make sense!

As I grieved, I could not eat nor drink unless someone brought it to me. I lost interest in everything I usually enjoyed and just sat on the couch all day looking at family photos of him. I was stuck trying to make sense of something that made no sense and stuck trying to reason something I didn't understand! Sure, I had plenty of loss prior to Kevin- the loss of relationships and the loss of things, but there's no loss quite like losing your soulmate, spouse, and best friend.

If you can relate to my story, I would like to share five steps inspired by scripture that helped me move forward to a place of hope:

1. Trust God
2. God is always in control
3. Purpose in the pain
4. Life after death
5. Our latter days can be greater

Trust God

It took about a month or so after losing my husband for me to begin reading my Bible again and seeking God for understanding. One day as I read, I heard the Lord say, "It's ok for you not to understand... just trust me." He then reminded me of my favorite Bible scripture, Proverbs 3:5-6:

*"Trust in the Lord with all your heart and **lean not on your own understanding**, in all your ways acknowledge Him and He will direct your path."*

For such a time as this, those words resonated in my spirit like never before. I realized that regardless of whether it made sense or not, I only needed to trust in God's perfect plan. He is the one who understands and knows what tomorrow will bring.

As I began to draw near to God again, His scriptures produced more sobering revelations, one of which came from 2 Corinthians 9:8-11. It assured me that the Lord was lifting and blessing me through the love of His good people. I was beginning to see beyond my pain, and I was so grateful.

God is always in control

A few months into my grieving process, when people would call to check on me, my response to them became, "All is well," not because I thought that's what they wanted to hear, but because I genuinely believed it. After talking with a friend, he reminded me of the story of the Shunammite woman in 2 Kings 4:8-37:

The story details the kindness and hospitality of the Shunammite woman to Elisha, the prophet. Because of her goodness toward him, he desired to bless her in return. When Elisha's servant, Gahazi, asked what she wanted, she answered that she was content. However, he noticed her husband was old, and she had no children. So, the prophet promised her a son within a year. She was excited and within that timeframe, she bo-

reason. Unfortunately, while helping his father with the harvest one year, he became ill and was sent home, where he died in his mother's arms. Even in her pain and suffering, she was still hopeful in the Lord, so she laid her son's body on Elisha's bed and set out to find him.

When her husband questioned her actions, she responded, "All is well." then she went on her way. When Elisha saw her coming, he asked his servant, Gahazi, to go to her and ask if everything was ok. When he did, she responded again, "All is well," and continued towards the prophet. Once she reached him she dropped to the ground and then clung to his feet asking:

"Why, would God give me a son that I didn't ask for just to take him away from me?"

It didn't make sense to her either.

But thankfully, this is not where the story ends. Elisha, the Shunammite Woman, and Gahazi returned to the room where the boy lay dead. Elisha then prayed to God and laid his body on top of the boy, and God raised him from the dead!

Just like the Shunammite woman, I too was expecting that God would turn this around, and heal my husband. But God had a different plan for Kevin and I. A plan that would be a major faith builder in my life.

Purpose in the pain.

During such emotional trauma, it almost seems impossible to fathom that there could be a purpose behind our pain.

We simply focus on just getting by the best we can without our loved one. Isn't it comforting to know that God is the author and finisher of our faith? God is able to purpose our pain. When we discover our passion out of our pain, we can begin to discover our purpose in life.

2 Corinthians 4 in the Amplified Bible reads:

"Therefore we do not become discouraged, spiritless, disappointed, or afraid. Though our outer self is progressively wasting away, yet our inner self is being progressively renewed day by day..."

I remember when the doctor first admitted my husband to the hospital and a nurse referred to me as his "caregiver." Her assessment of my role in his life opened my eyes to it because I never saw myself as a caregiver. I saw myself as being the devoted wife that I vowed to be. This experience became an "Ah-Ha" moment for me that opened my spiritual eyes. While past hurts began to resurface, I discovered that all of my pain had produced a passion for helping others who were also hurting.

I further surmised that as God had me to walk alongside my husband during his illness, He was stretching me for a larger purpose. I can easily see why my heart desires to help both hurting men and women, caregivers, widows, and widowers.

Life after death

It's so important to allow yourself the freedom to grieve in your own way. A word of advice; don't let others dictate to you your process.

For me, I had to give myself permission to grieve in my own way.

No one should try to tell you what that looks like for you or how long it should take you. It is an individual process. Only God knows and can truly walk through your process with you. Psalm 147:3 (Amplified Bible reminds us:

"He heals the brokenhearted and binds up their wounds healing their pain and comforting their sorrow."

During my process, I have felt in shock, depressed, confused, scared, angry, hurt, lonely and in denial. There were even times I experienced many or all these emotions in one week! This is what I mean by "allowing ourselves the freedom to go through the process in our own unique way without any judgment from others or ourselves." There are several contributing factors that helped me through my process of grief: my faith, my covenant marriage, walking along side my husband during his illness, and the support I received from my friends, family and the church.

All of these things helped me to see how God is in control of every aspect of our lives and how He can take us from a place of grief to a place of hope.

Our latter days can be greater

One morning after reading the Word and praying, I can recall how the Lord put a song on my heart. The song is called "I Can See Clearly Now" by Johnny Nash.

I thought that it was unusual because I only had heard it a few times and didn't really know the song.

I immediately grabbed my iPad and looked up the song because I didn't know the name of the song nor who sang it. Once I figured it out, I looked up the lyrics to read them as I listened to the song.

Here are the lyrics:

"I Can See Clearly Now" by Johnny Nash

I can see clearly now the rain is gone
I can see all obstacles in my way
Gone are the dark clouds that had me blind
It's gonna be a bright, bright sun shiny day

I think I can make it now the pain is gone
All of the bad feelings have disappeared
Here is that rainbow I've been praying for
It's gonna be a bright, bright sun shiny day

Look all around, there's nothing but blue skies
Look straight ahead, nothing but blue skies

I can see clearly now, the rain is gone
I can see all obstacles in my way
Gone are the dark clouds that had me blind
It's gonna be a bright, bright sun shiny day

As the song played, it brought me to tears...tears of hope and joy. God revealed 3 things to me through this song:

1. The pain will get easier because He is the healer of the broken-hearted.
2. Look towards what is ahead and press on towards the goal for my life.
3. The future will be bright as a sunny day because my latter days can be better than ever!

I realized then again how much God loves me...so much that He would speak to me through an old song to remind me that all is well. God is so faithful!

I know it's hard to imagine that a loss of this magnitude could be a part of what God can use in our lives to bless us and others... He can, but only if we see our circumstances through our spiritual eyes that enlightens us to what God is doing. I asked myself, "What if a part of my journey from when I said 'I Do' to where I currently am is necessary for reaching my full potential and walking into my purpose?" God began to deepen my faith in Him.

Regardless of what God is doing, He can use it all, because **all things** work together for the good of those who love him, who are called according to His purpose. (Romans 8:28. He doesn't use just the pretty and pleasant things, He can use anything He chooses! This should give us comfort because God is in control and has a plan to prosper us and not to harm us, plans to give us hope and a future, according to Jeremiah 29:11.

Because God is the protector of widows, we can move forward from grief towards our healing.

I couldn't imagine getting to this point in the process so soon, but when I heard God's response to my prayer for understanding, I shifted from being "stuck" to being "shifted towards joy"! I no longer question God's timing because I realize now that even when it doesn't make sense, His timing is perfect!

Blessed is the woman who trusts in the Lord, whose hope is in Him. For she will be like a tree planted by the water, sending its roots out toward a stream. She doesn't fear when heat comes because her leaves remain green. She doesn't worry when the drought comes because she bears fresh fruit in every season.
Jeremiah 17: 7-8

All is Well!

About Marlo Beamon

Marlo Beamon is a Massachusetts native who currently resides in Acworth, GA, just outside of Atlanta. She is a Minister, Life, Growth and Leadership Coach, and the owner of Divine Designz, where she crafts original jewelry pieces.

In 1999 she married her loving husband, Kevin, whom she co-labored with and launched "Word of Faith Community Church." They were married for over 20 years before the Lord took him home in March of 2020.

Today, Marlo seeks to help hurting people worldwide and those who struggle with the loss of their loved ones.

Connect with Marlo Beamon at ladybeamon10@gmail.com

BOOMERANG

BY PATRICE CALDWELL-GABRIEL

Boomerang

About a year ago, I was awakened by the presence of the Lord. Into the calm of my spirit, He whispered, "Book and Chris." I paused at that moment and then listened intently to see what God would reveal next. The thing was, God did not say anything else, and I did not question him.

Diagnosis/Chemo

In October 2015, a year before Christopher's cancer prognosis, he complained about pain in his stomach and side and went to the emergency room in excruciating agony. The x-rays revealed gallstones, and we were sent home with medication to assist in passing the stones. He got better but never felt entirely well. Over the next several months, he kept complaining about being very tired and not having any energy. Then I remembered that he was several years late getting his colonoscopy. I kept telling him to schedule an appointment with his physician, and he responded each time he did not want to take off from work.

How often do we hear this from men when it comes to their well-being? I kept insisting that he see a doctor but to no avail. So, one year later, on October sixteenth, we find ourselves in the emergency room again. This time they admit him, take x-rays and do blood work. The results of the x-rays showed lesions on his colon. They suggested we set-up an appointment with an Oncologist.

At first, there was a flurry of thoughts that eventually assembled into total disbelief. I could also hear a voice in my head warning me not to panic and questioning how we got here?

We took the next step and set the appointment. During the wait-time, I felt anxious and dazed by unbelief, yet I prayed, "Lord, please show us favor."

When the day and time came for his appointment, I was working as a traveling Sales Consultant on assignment in New York. I went to my hotel room to have a private three-way conference call about my husband's condition. However, I was not prepared for what the doctor said. In very formal medical terms, he concluded that Christopher had Stage IV Colon Cancer.

My mind blacked out for a moment. I was in shock and extremely choked up. I managed to make it through the call with tears rolling down my face because I had to be strong for Chris.

When the call ended, I told my husband I would call him back. I then shared Christopher's test results with my colleague and friend and left work shortly after. I needed to process what I heard. When I finally made it back into my hotel room, let me tell you, I totally lost it!

After I got myself together, I called Chris back, and we cried and prayed together. Then, we agreed to stand like soldiers ready to fight. He said, "Me and you against the world babe- Team Caldwell!"

Then we built a foundation of positive energy, faith, prayer, and love.

The Treatment Process Begins

Christopher started his Chemotherapy, and for the first month or so, it worked, and we constantly received great reports. However, those results were short-lived. The medicine started causing some side effects that could potentially lead to permanent damage, so they decided to try another medication. The new medicine was not working, and we became discouraged but still believed for a miracle.

Giving up was not an option.

Our Love

After seventeen years of being single, I met the man of my dreams. Our introduction took place on a dating site in October of 2011. His profile stated he was from Detroit, MI but currently living in Atlanta, GA. He was a six-foot, one, 300-pound truck driver with a spiritual profile detailing his desire for a partner. We talked all night long; I think I had 2 hours of sleep before I had to go to work. Inside I felt so unbelievably happy!

A few weeks later, he came to visit for the weekend. I had several friends on standby to make sure I did not come up missing. Even now, I smile when I think of my security crew. Anyway, I remember driving around the airport looking for the man in the dating profile. At the same time, he was giving me instructions on the phone, of where to meet him. So, I kept driving until I saw this really attractive guy on the phone. His lips were moving in response to my questions, and I realized it was him. I pulled over, exited the car, and greeted him with a big smile and a warm hug, an embrace he called a church hug. When he got in the car, all I could say was, "Oh my God, you are so cute!" I must have said it all day.

Needless to say, the weekend went very well. Christopher went home and immediately started planning to move to Dallas. After four months of dating, we became husband and wife on February eighteenth, 2012. I was over the moon with excitement to be Mrs. Christopher Caldwell. I was totally in love with this man, and we were so perfect for one another.

I was looking forward to spending the rest of my life with this wonderful man. He was my hero, my best friend, and my joy in times of sorrow. We traveled together and spent an enormous amount of time with friends and family. Everyone that knew him knew he was an incredibly special person.

Death

Christopher called me at work to let me know the doctors said there was nothing else they could do. My manager was already aware of what we were facing, so when I shared the news, she was heartbroken and helped me get home. When I arrived, he was sobbing and apologizing for having to leave me.

That's when I reached out to the Cancer Treatment Center of America for another opinion. Several days later, we flew to Philadelphia. Once there, he took a turn for the worse, and they immediately admitted him. Doctors ordered tests and then gathered to discuss a plan of action. Unfortunately, the final diagnosis was there was nothing else they could do.

The cancer had spread over 75 percent of his colon. They predicted he only had a short time to live, and I was devastated. I held it together in front of him long enough to make it to one of the private prayer rooms. Then I cried a river! How could this be? We only shared five short years together. We always talked about living a long life together until we had gray hair (me, not him, because he was bald). We would hold hands while sitting in rocking chairs and smiling with gums smooth as a baby bottom.

Now, with all these unexpected changes, there were arrangements to be made. First, we sold our home, and I flew back to Dallas to pack up for the move. I was not happy because it meant spending less time with Christopher. We decided that he would spend his last days in Detroit with his children, family, and most of his friends. With that being settled, his best friend and his wife flew to Philadelphia to accompany Christopher back to Detroit. Boy, what a lifesaver!

They delivered him safely to his sister and brother-in-law's home, who welcomed him to live out his days. She would have it no other way.

I was scheduled to fly to Detroit in 5 days. However, his niece called and said he was getting fussy and belligerent. He kept asking for me. They kept telling him I was coming, but eventually, he got agitated and screamed, "WHERE IS MY WIFE?" You guys keep telling me she is coming! So, his niece called to see if there was any way I could get there sooner.

Fortunately, I was able to get an earlier flight and called to let him know I was coming. He was so excited that he took his own shower by himself. He ate well and slept in the regular bed instead of his hospital bed. My flight arrived at midnight. Shortly after, I walked into Christopher's room filled with family and close friends. He was peacefully resting. I sat next to him and began caressing his face before I spoke so I would not startle him. He immediately sat up and embraced me tight for quite a while. It felt like an out of body experience; Christopher's true love for me was definitely shown at that moment. There was not a dry eye in the room.

Within the next couple of days, the house was a revolving door with folks coming to spend time with him. He held on to make sure he saw his children and grandchildren. The night before he passed, he asked his niece to pray over him. She draped her prayer cloth over him, and we all gathered in prayer. Shortly after, he started to experience shortness of breath, and we employed his oxygen machine. He then relaxed peacefully. On June fifteenth, 2017, his final curtain closed. There is no preparation when you hear the words, "He is gone." I was truly beside myself.

Christopher David Caldwell - December twenty-fifth, 1961 – June fifteenth, 2017.

The levels of immense sadness and loss caused me to feel numb and like no one understood my pain.

Memorials

Now it was time to start the funeral arrangements. Mentally, I was not fully present but knew I had to push through. Unaware, however as always Chris had resolved the matter for me. The previous week Chris reached out to the funeral director and conveyed his wishes to be cremated. He also, shared with close family members that under no circumstances was ANYONE to give his wife a hard time about his decisions.

My immediate thoughts were of his unconditional love for me and how he wanted to make this process as stress-free as possible.

Colleagues flew in and drove for miles to provide support. Their presence was unexpected and touched my heart. I was grateful.

Both memorials; Detroit and Dallas were executed in the manner he requested.

Mourning Process

Now it was time to go through not having my love with me on this side of life. The pain that pierced my heart and soul was unbearable. I felt utterly lost. My heart ached so bad some days I did not know if I would make it. Still, my faith was strong, and I know that we all have this path to cross one day but, ooh wee! I did not want to deal with this. Not now! All I kept asking myself, is what am I going to do? Lord, help me! ! It is so hard to explain the pain I felt. I was so empty. For the first year, I slept a lot and could not find the energy to get out of bed. I cried constantly and prayed like no other. At times I fell into depression, isolated myself, and could not eat. Dealing with holidays, birthdays, and new births without him was the hardest. But Christmas was the worst because that was his birthday too.

Restoration Process

The third month after his passing, I realized I had to push past the pain and get myself together. I am a structured person, so I started incorporating a plan to go back to work. The preparation included:

- Reciting scriptures on healing, faith, and peace.
- Setting a time to get out of bed, brush my teeth, shower, and put clothes on rather I left the house or not. (This was really hard.)
- Listening to spiritual, uplifting, and encouraging sermons.
- Praise and Worship to some of my favorite gospel singers.
- Pray.
- Talk to Chris's Urn; it gave me a sense of peace.
- Listen to voice messages to hear his voice.
- Allow myself to cry because afterward, I received peace.
- Look at videos of my husband. I cried, but it was ok, because, again, I received peace.

- Always talk about him to any and everyone who would listen. I did not care if it annoyed people or not. It gave me peace.

Each day got better than the day before. I was never hard on myself about how long my healing process should take, no matter how others felt. I had to run the course and continue the process. As I wrote this section, I cried and wiped snot like a baby with a bad cold. But it is ok. I found peace.

A **Boomerang** is a flat, curved tool designed to be thrown like a frisbee. The only difference is a boomerang returns to the point from whence it came.

So, with a proverbial Boomerang in our hands, Chris and I became airborne, sailing on life and love, but when death struck, the Boomerang returned only to me. I felt as if my life shattered but little did I know a blessing was around the corner, and I would begin again.

New Love

In the fall of 2019, I received a call early one morning from a very, close friend while away on a work assignment.

She said, "Girl, this morning, my husband woke up and said, what do you think about Larry and your friend Patrice?"

My friend responded to her husband, "Hmm. I think you might have something there."

Turning over her suggestion in my mind, I remembered that Larry was a tender widower of 4 months. I had been widowed for 2 years.

Nevertheless, they invited us to a tailgate event upon my return to Dallas. I accepted the invitation, and with my grandson in tow Larry and I were introduced. Right away I could see a connection between Larry and my grandchild that let me know he was a great guy. We too connected with much conversation which evolved into a short courtship. On Thanksgiving Eve, Larry proposed, and, on January twentieth, 2020, we married privately in a fine dining facility. In attendance were 40 of our closest friends and family. I am so grateful that God saw fit to give me another chance at love.

For me, single life was not an option. Through God's faithfulness finding true love again is possible when your heart and soul are ready. To God, be the Glory!

About Patrice Caldwell-Gabriel

Patrice Caldwell-Gabriel is a California native who grew up in Watts, California. In addition to being a devoted Woman of Faith, Wife, Mother, and Grandmother, she is on a spiritual journey nurtured by the word of God. Currently, she thrives as an Independent National Hotel/ Hospitality Sales Executive, the CEO of PMC Trucking, LLC Logistics Company, and a Skilled Credit Repair Consultant.

Mrs. Gabriel is a stepmother to the children of her late husband, Christopher David Caldwell, and has since found love and marriage, once again with current husband, Larry Gabriel.

Connect with Patrice Caldwell-Gabriel at patriceewell66@gmail.com

A WIDOWS PEAK

BY VERONICA CORBETT WEST

My relationship with my Husband is where my journey of Resilience began.

On the second Sunday in August of 1993, what should have been a routine walk to the choir stand became a detour to my destiny. You see, amid my stride, I noticed a nice-looking man with whom I exchanged pleasantries. I would later learn that he was our new Minister of Music and on fire for the Lord! Furthermore, he used his gift to teach and play with excellence. As time went on and at the urging of my best friend, our pleasantries became conversations. Eventually, we started dating, and by September of 1995, I was Mrs. John Michael West.

Hello. My name is Veronica Corbett West, and the story I'm about to share is just one amongst the many women who have "loved and lost." If I could categorize my journey between the "loving and the losing," it would read, "Resilience." This is a word I have become intimately familiar with... It is a word that I turn to for answers that would otherwise elude me. Its definition is, "The ability of a substance or object to spring back into shape; elasticity." ...I have certainly been stretched.

My relationship with my husband is where my journey of Resilience began. The word "Peak" in the title indicates the most crucial level that I have had to face thus far, and that was the last 11 days of Michael's life. Today, I share my story by inviting you into my faith, pain, acceptance, and resilience.

Saturday, December 16, 2006

My husband and I rose at 5am for morning prayer. Afterward, he went to his standing appointment with the barber, and I, to a luncheon celebrating my father's retirement. While at the event, I received a phone call from Michael inquiring about my return home. The nature of the call was very concerning because he needed me to take him to Urgent Care. I paused because I never knew him to be the guy who would make such a request. For many years he worked in a hospital emergency room and would seek treatment at work when needed. Even during those instances, he would share the situation with me after the fact.

When I arrived home, he was in the dining room looking through some paperwork. It would be days later when I'd realize the significance of his search. The tests in Urgent Care revealed that his kidneys were not functioning at an acceptable level. It would be necessary to admit him to the main hospital for further diagnostics.

Sunday, December 17, 2006

I arrived home from the hospital around 3am, got up at 5am for Morning Prayer but didn't go to Church. Instead, I reached out to his mother, who lived in another state.

I also called my parents and our siblings to make them aware of what we knew thus far. Afterward, I drove his car to the hospital, noticing he'd been listening to Walter Hawkins, "Love Alive 5" CD. The song playing was, "Is There Any Way?" Tears began to stream down my face as the lyrics resonated in my spirit.

"Knowing it was really You who carried me right on through some tears and some pain, But I'm going on just the same. God, you promised to be with me through the storm and through the rain. God, you are my everything."

I spent the rest of the day at the hospital fielding calls from concerned family and friends and greeting visitors from our church. Both of us were uneasy because we didn't know what would come next. Still, we believed that he would emerge victoriously.

Monday, December 18, 2006

A few weeks prior, I'd started a new job with the Detroit Public School system. These would be the last few days of work before the Christmas break. As usual, I got up at 5am for Morning Prayer. My husband and I already agreed that I should not jeopardize my probation status by missing work. So, I kept our agreement and phoned him throughout the day. On one of those calls, he shared that the doctors were planning to start him on dialysis. They were hopeful that his condition would be temporary and reverse itself with medication. I shared the update with our parents, siblings, and Pastor. Then after work, I spent the next several hours visiting with him at the hospital.

Tuesday, December 19, 2006

Tuesday morning greeted me for prayer time and later with a plan to leave work early because his dialysis was scheduled for noon. I didn't want him to be alone due to his palpable anxiety about the procedure. So, imagine my relief when his Godmother called and told me she could be there with him. After work, I spent the next several hours visiting with him and found that day one of dialysis had gone well. Yet, we were both praying that he would not need it indefinitely.

Wednesday, December 20, 2006

I had been exhausted ever since taking him to Urgent Care four days ago. However, I still rose at 5am, fasting until 5pm, to align myself corporately with our Church. In the coming days, I would realize the impact of the righteous, effectual, and fervent prayers.

The phone rang shortly after prayer. It was the hospital telling me that during the night, Michael had experienced difficulty breathing. Therefore, he'd been taken to the Intensive Care Unit. It was now the last day of work before the Christmas break, but I already knew that I would not be able to work. So, I called my boss and updated my mother-in-law en route to the hospital. I would call the others once I had more information.

When I arrived at the hospital, I went to his original room to gather his personal items, spoke with the doctors, and spent the rest of the day by his side.

Thursday, December 21, 2006

The second day of his dialysis found me in my familiar posture of prayer. Afterward, I went to the hospital, pretty much repeating the routine from the day before. Only, this time, he was on oxygen but in good spirits. We even joked about how he had gotten a manicure a few weeks earlier and then came home, angrily searching for nail polish remover. It seemed that his nail technician had been in a hurry to finish and mistakenly used a tinted polish. I told him that when he went to sleep tonight, I would use an iridescent polish on his nails, and he smiled. We were both still believing God for his condition to be temporary. We then prayed together, and I went home that night.

Friday, December 22, 2006

After the 5am prayer, I dressed and went to the hospital, grateful that he didn't have to endure dialysis today. We discussed the special church service taking place that evening, and he urged me to go. I promised him I would return as soon as the service ended, then left because I needed the encouragement and strength. When I returned, he was resting but woke up briefly to ask, "How were the Dancers?" I then shared what a blessing the service had been, we prayed, and then I went home around midnight. That would be the last conversation we ever held.

Saturday, December 23, 2006

The hospital called before morning prayer and asked me to come right away because he had developed Sepsis. The doctor's decision was to place my husband in a medically induced coma to give his body a chance to fight the infection.

While en route, I called his mother and shared his condition with her. She, being a nurse by profession, had a better understanding of what was taking place. I learned later that she realized the gravity of the situation but didn't want to alarm me. She simply said that she was packing a suitcase and was on her way to the airport.

When I arrived at the hospital, he was not awake, but I believed that he would hear me if I anointed him and prayed. He had cheated death twice before, and I had faith that God would bring him through this situation.

Sunday, December 24, 2006

After morning prayer, I went to the hospital prepared to spend Sunday with my husband. It was a given that he would never miss church if he was able to be there. So, I took my Bible, and although he could not respond, I read scriptures about healing and restoration. I then anointed him again and prayed. His mother arrived in town that evening, and we spoke by phone about his unvarying condition.

Monday, December 25, 2006

After morning prayer on Christmas Day, I stopped by my parent's house on my way to the hospital. Thus far, his condition had not changed. Nevertheless, his loved ones stopped by, and his mother and I took turns with him in-between visits. Around 8pm, the doctors spoke to his mother and me privately. His condition had worsened, his organs were shutting down, and they had one more medication they would try to reverse his current state. When they followed with "...an 85 percent chance that he would not survive the night," I went numb.

His mother and I both left the private meeting in silence. There was a great cloud of visitors in the waiting room, but neither of us spoke to anyone. In fact, my mother-in-law, a mighty praying woman, walked away because she needed to hear from God. I went immediately to the elevator and down to the first floor. Once outside, I sat on a bench near the emergency room entrance. It was dark, cold, and began to snow. Pondering the situation before me, I took a deep breath, looked up into the sky, and audibly told God that I accept His Will being done in this matter. When I returned, my mother, sister, and best friend waited to pray with me in the chapel. It was there that I found the strength to tell them about the doctor's prognosis. Shortly after breaking the news, his mother and I were called urgently into his room. He had coded once, but they were able to bring him back. His mother and I talked and decided that if he coded again, not to resuscitate.

Tuesday, December 26, 2006

Just after midnight, my mother-in-law and I were called into his room once again. We both knew the end was near. As I held his hand, he took his last breath at 12:15am.

This was my *peak*, my darkest hour, and in it, God gave me a peace that surpassed all understanding. I believe the reservoir of my strength and resolve flowed from the corporate prayer during December. While driving home early that morning, I could feel God's presence as the CD in the car played, "Is there Any Way?" I remember thanking God for the reminder that He would never leave nor forsake me. Now, inside the stillness of my home, I realized what he had been looking for before I took him to Urgent Care. There, on the table, near the stack of papers, he had placed his picture. At that moment I remembered that I had gotten him a new suit for his birthday in May. He was always quite a dresser... A few months prior, he put the suit together with a shirt, tie, and handkerchief and insisted that I see how it looked. Although he never shared it, I believe he knew "death would soon part us." Ultimately, I used that photo on the front of his obituary, and I dressed him just as he showed me.

Life After Death

Sitting in my new reality of being a 37-year-old widow without children gave me some dark thoughts. I was unsure of what my existence would be without him. His ministry had consumed much of our lives, and I was saddened by thoughts of being lonely and unloved. But, fortunately, God gave me a wonderful family, close friends, and some dynamic people in my life. They have nurtured me and spoken into my spirit. Even my first Pastor, who has gone on to be with the Lord, spoke to my heart about what it truly means to be a widow. My then Pastor, above all, changed my perspective... He spoke boldly into my spirit of Resilience by saying, "Michael had to die so that you could live."

After coming to grips with that statement, I started to feel OK about living. I believed that not only do I deserve to be loved but that I will love again. That revelation was a well-spring that gave me strength and a Word for others who have lost their spouse. I always tell them, "It is an experience that you will never forget, but as time goes on, your grief will become easier to manage."

I remind them that their marriage vow has been fulfilled and God will honor them.

For me, it's been 14 years since Michael died. Still, in December, I always think of the last 11 days of his life. That is when the gift of my resilience abounds, and my circumstances become powerless to define me. That is when I trust God more and believe even harder...That is when I get excited about what my future holds.

About Veronica Corbett West, MBA/MAED

Veronica Corbett West and her younger sister were raised on Detroit's Westside. However, the family originally hails from The Carolina's. Mrs. West has a MBA in several categories of Management, Administration and Adult Education..

Her multi-faceted career spans more than 30 years and includes:

- Graphic Design and Printing
- Human Resources
- Training and Development
- Customer Service, and much more.

On September 30, 1995, Veronica married John Michael West who sadly passed away December 26, 2006, at the age of 39. In the years since her husband's death, Mrs. West pondered ways to help others who struggled with losing a spouse. Fortunately, her desire was fulfilled when the opportunity to contribute her personal account of widowhood to *"A Widow's Resilience."*

Connect with Veronica Corbett West at msveedub@gmail.com

SOULFUL MOURNING

BY KIKO DAVIS SNODDY

Soulful Mourning

Before I married my late husband, Don Davis, he confided that for years he planned to retire from his successful business empire, sell everything that held him down, and take off to see every part of the planet he hadn't explored. He wanted to experience the different cultures, music, art, and history. He wanted to breathe different air.

From the mid-1950s until 1980, Don actively enjoyed a wildly successful career in the music industry. His wealth of achievements included being a three-time Grammy Award-winning songwriter, Billboard Magazine Producer of the Year, musician, manager, publisher, and studio owner. He worked with some of the top names in the music business, such as Aretha Franklin, The Four Tops, The Dells, Johnny Taylor, Anita Baker, and many more.

However, by 1980 the music landscape had changed to Disco, which didn't fit the Grammy Winners style. Deciding to bow out of the music industry, Don set his eyes on another opportunity-the acquisition of the then-struggling First Independence Bank in Detroit, Michigan.

This endeavor would allow him to utilize his business penchant for turning things into gold literally.

First Independence Bank was established in 1970 by a group of prominent black business owners and pastors. Their alliance resulted from the racial injustice and economic inequality that spurred the 1967 Detroit Rebellion. By 1980 the bank was struggling financially and in need of serious capital. It was then that Don Davis's purpose became clear as an opportunity to save the bank and start a new chapter in his already prolific life.

Just like that, Don Davis left the music business and became the CEO and owner of First Independence Bank. Not only did he manage to save FIB, but he also built the institution into an overwhelming financial success.

For Don, all was going as planned. His assets included a thriving banking empire, multiple business entities, and plenty of toys and trinkets. On top of that, he was a happily confirmed bachelor who was married to his career. That type of ambition left little time for anyone or anything else. At 63 years old, Don was convinced he would ride out the rest of his days in blissful bachelorhood, and he was fine with that until the afternoon we met.

I was a realtor he was interviewing to sell his private residence. He was looking to minimize his living space and personal effects in preparation for his adventure around the world. We agreed to meet at a restaurant where I arrived twenty minutes early-

You see, I was eager to make a good impression, because I really wanted to land his multi-million-dollar listing. I had come close in the past, yet, this time I felt in my spirit, I would be successful.

Don, on the other hand, arrived twenty minutes late, well dressed with a disarming smile. As he approached the table, I stood to extend my hand; however, he dismissed the gesture, choosing to cup my face with both hands instead.

"What a face, what a face," he said tenderly.

Ordinarily, I would've viewed this as being inappropriate; yet I was totally at ease and enveloped by a feeling of warmth. Much later, Don would share that he knew I would become his wife. Maybe that explained why I immediately felt at home in his presence.

Not realizing that I was being interviewed for far more than a realtor's position, I proceeded to offer him a dossier of my expertise and comparative market analysis reports. Graciously, he entertained my professionalism before asking me about my personal goals, dreams, and aspirations.

I was floored; usually, clients didn't ask questions like that. He was sincere and listened intently. After some time, he began to share his life story with me. I was so mesmerized by the glitz, glamour, drama, and heartache; I didn't realize three hours had passed. I reminded myself that although our meeting was scintillating, I needed to stay on task.

Therefore, I asked him If I could tour his property to make a more in-depth analysis of its market value? He said yes. With a sigh of relief, I realized I made it past the initial interview. I was the fifth realtor he considered and the first to make it to Stage II.

His residence was only ten minutes away from the restaurant, so we decided that I would follow his lead in my car. The scenic route of winding roads hugging crystal lakes accentuated homes ranging from charming to majestic. It was all so absolutely breathtaking and romantic I had to keep telling myself, "Focus, Focus! You are here for a payday, not a playdate!" - and it worked, for a while...

Meanwhile, we arrived at his contemporary Tobocman home, where I marveled at the stunning lakeside masterpiece! Don dismissed himself to take a conference call, leaving me to survey the property, and take notes and photos. I was to meet back with him in an hour to discuss my assessment. Upon his departure, I began my journey outside, taking note of the beautifully manicured grounds, tennis courts, greenhouse, guesthouse, and eight-car garage. There was a serene lake with sailboats gliding by, complete with two white swans nestled together; again romantic, again, telling myself to get my head out of the clouds- "you have a job to do!"

I move back inside, noting the interior was equally impressive, embellished with gorgeous travertine marble flooring and walls. Raw silk texturized the elegant powder room while floor-to-ceiling windows framed incredible lake views. The kitchen was a chef's dream and the mahogany wood-paneled library a masterpiece. By the time I reached the luxurious master bedroom, my review was nearly complete, and everything seemed fine- that is until I walked into the master closet. Suddenly I felt warm and light-headed, needing to perch on a nearby ottoman. Thankfully, the feeling soon passed, and I continued taking photos while admiring Don's fine haberdashery. His expansive collection had me feeling like a little girl in a fantasy, as I felt compelled to touch the various fabrics, and smell the cologne. It was at that moment I realized half the closet was empty. Without even thinking, I said out loud, "Don't worry, Mr. Davis, I will fill the empty space in your closet with my shoes!" And, just like that, I went back to his office, gave him my review, and asked him If he would give me the listing. After a brief pause, he replied yes.

Don thought we should celebrate and offered me a glass of wine; I declined; however, I did accept grape juice instead. We began talking, and two hours later, the sun was setting. It was clear he was smitten, and so was I; nevertheless, I excused myself from the chaise lounge by the fireplace to go to the bathroom. Once inside, I threw water on my face and said, "Young lady, get yourself out of here, keep it professional!" So, I did.

Returning to his office, I informed Mr. Davis, that I had a prior engagement (I didn't) and must be on my way! He was visibly disappointed, nonetheless a consummate gentleman, apologizing for keeping me so long.

Additionally, he gave me several phone numbers of where he could be reached — all for business purposes, of course. By the time I hustled back to the winding road, it was dark outside, and I had all the signs of a schoolgirl crush. It didn't help that the moonlight was glistening on the lake. Still, I wasn't ready to accept my reality just yet.

The very next day, Don called me to say he had a friend who wanted to buy a home and several others looking for commercial properties. This exchange would launch the next several weeks of consistent communication under the guise of business referrals. Ultimately quite a few dinners and lunches took place where he would make the necessary introductions. One evening he asked me to meet him for dinner, and when I arrived, I was surprised to see him alone. I became nervous, thinking one of the referrals was unhappy but he just wanted to speak with me alone. I listened cautiously as Don talked about his life journey, sharing many reflective moments from his storied past. Then he reached a point where he paused for a bit, gazed at me, and then plainly said, I love you!

I was shocked by his profession of love but also relieved. I felt the same way, but I would've never admitted it to anyone, not even myself. Yet, truthfully, for the last six weeks, all I did was think of him. I barely slept, keeping it all inside out of fear my feelings were not justified or appropriate because he was my client. He told me he couldn't sleep or really eat, either and it blew me away. At that moment, he leaned over and gently kissed my forehead, and I knew I was a goner. From that day forward, we were inseparable.

Several weeks later, three days before Christmas 2002, he asked when I would be ready to marry him? I told him when the time is right, you will know it!

Our relationship was an answered prayer because I had previously asked God to send my husband and best friend; I was very specific as I wanted a true soulmate. I even cut out pictures of places we would travel, the home we would share, and photos of adorable children we would have, and placed them in my Bible. These keepsakes were to be forgotten until our wedding day, which would be a year and a few months later.

Our married life, just like our courtship, was spiritually, emotionally, and psychically rewarding for both of us! We traveled extensively to exotic locations, attended many cultural events and concerts; you name it, we did it together! We spent countless hours talking about everything you could imagine. Two years into our marriage, our beautiful daughter Skye Adonna arrived, and eighteen months following, we were blessed again with our son, Don Jr.

Don was over the moon! He finally had what he'd been yearning for, his own family. The four of us settled into a lifestyle that centered around our children. We rarely went anywhere without our two little shadows. Don would go on long walks, too strenuous for tiny toddler legs, so he would put them in a wagon and pull them along. Even when we would go to the Caribbean, renting luxurious oceanfront villas, the children would tag along with us. If a business trip required him to be away more than three days, he would insist the children and I come along. I never complained as it was usually someplace near the ocean or a beach. This pattern of togetherness and family would be constant throughout our marriage.

As the children went off to school, I went back to work, and eventually, Don and I began to partner on real estate ventures and business projects. It was a great feeling to have his business expertise, total support, and respect.

By the end of 2012, Don began to speak of winding down his banking career; he wanted to travel and spend more time with the children and me. Of course, I was in total agreement. He began making plans to delegate some of his duties and strategize the next phase of his life. By spring of 2013, he wasn't totally out of the game just yet, but he was noticeably clocking fewer hours and traveling a bit more. To our delight, in May of 2013, we took a weeklong cruise to the Caribbean with our children and our favorite cousins from Atlanta, the Kelly Family. For the first few days, we had an amazing time celebrating each night at dinner and going on exciting excursions each day. However, by the third day of the cruise, Don started to experience pain in his shoulder. I didn't think much of it; perhaps putting Skye on his shoulders as he often did was a contributing factor. On the fourth day, he declined to get off the ship.

"Boy, you must have really overdone it!" I said urging him to get a massage. He complied and felt better for a day or two but by the end of the cruise, the pain returned, and he chalked it up to old age.

For several months after our cruise Don would take multiple trips to the doctor including a chiropractor. At times he would seem okay; at others, he would be in visible pain. I began to think the pain resulted from a pinched nerve; Don agreed with that possibility and pursued multiple therapies to ease his pain. Although he continued to work through his increasing discomfort, he didn't do much socializing or after-work events, he did, however, continue to go on long walks.

On July 2, Don walked into the house with his nose bleeding, and a scrape on his arm. I asked, "What happened?" He told me he tripped over the hose at the gas station while pumping gas.

"Wow, are you okay?" He replied yes, as he limped into the bedroom. The rest of the weekend, we stayed in, and I attended to his wounds. Monday came, and he said he wasn't going into the office. I dropped the children at school and returned home to find Don in the kitchen grabbing a snack. Something didn't seem quite right; his balance was off, and he still seemed to be in pain. A short time later, he told me he was leaving to go to an appointment. Noticing that he still seemed to be off-balanced, I mentioned he didn't look well and probably should stay home and rest. Of course, he protested, claiming he was just fine, but as he headed out the door, I followed, insisting on driving him. He must have been in a lot of pain because he didn't stop me from grabbing the keys.

As I backed out of the driveway, I asked where we were going? "To the hospital," he responded.

I was somewhat surprised yet, kind of relieved; maybe now we could get to the source of his pain and find some form of relief. When we arrived at the hospital, he directed me where to park, and as we walked, there were multiple signs with arrows indicating the various medical departments. Don appeared to know where he was going, so I followed closely by his side. Soon we arrived at the reception desk, checked in, and were instructed to have a seat. About 15 minutes later, we were called back to an examination room where a nurse came in and took his vitals. Afterward, a courteous doctor appeared.

"Hello, Mr. Davis, good to see you again!"

"Again?" I questioned- "He's been here before?" The doctor then studied Don's face and arm, noticing the various scrapes and scratches.

"What happened to your face?" he asked.

"I tripped over the hose at the gas station," Don said. "It's not a big deal; I get a little off-balance sometimes. The doctor looked at him and proceeded to have Don do a series of strength tests. He then looked over his charts a bit and said, "It's the cancer attacking your nerves."

"My heart stopped! I couldn't breathe. My mind was racing, and immediately, I felt nauseous. The shock held my rationale hostage — I didn't know what to say — It didn't matter because I couldn't speak. I just sat there, not really accepting the reality of what I was hearing. I looked over at Don, who had a blank look on his face.

He needed my support, so I composed myself by bottling up my emotions. The doctor went on advising about various treatment options, recommending that he choose one quickly because his cancer was Stage IV.

"What? Stage IV?" my thoughts screamed! "This can't be!"

I grabbed my chest to keep my heart from escaping! Both the doctor and my beloved husband saw my reaction. The doctor appeared uncomfortable as he realized Don had not shared the news with me. I reached for Don's hand, trying to compose myself, and squeezed hard. I didn't say a word when I really wanted to scream, "Why is this happening? I felt powerless. As the visit came to an end, the doctor advised Don to expeditiously get back with his decision.

The silence was thick the entire ride home. Neither of us spoke because we were both hurting. Of course, I wanted to know why my husband hadn't told me about the cancer diagnosis; I also knew the "why" would have to take a backseat.

That evening I catered to his every need; not pressing, but instead allowing him the mental space to just be. He played a bit with the children, had dinner, and retired to the bedroom early to watch TV. I showered and climbed into bed next to him. He pulled me close and held me tight. At that moment, I said, I love you, we will survive this, we must pray! He kissed me on my forehead and said, "I know." We prayed and drifted off to sleep in each other's arms.

Don decided on a combination of treatments and, within a few days, began the process. At first, the side effects were minimal and didn't impede our daily routines. However, as time rolled on, the treatments and disease began to take a toll on his physical appearance. He was losing weight and couldn't walk very far without experiencing extreme fatigue. On top of it all, Don didn't like to discuss his condition and didn't want anyone else to know. These restrictions were extremely difficult, yet I wanted to be a source of comfort and continuous support, so I complied. He preferred to hear about the children, my daily activities, and lighter, happier subjects. He was already in pain; I didn't want to add to it.

Inside, I was experiencing extreme emotional anguish, anxiety, and stress. To say I was overwhelmed would be a gross understatement. The decline in my husband's health coupled with taking care of our five and seven-year-old children directed me inward. Therefore, I began to rise at 5:00 am to kneel and say a specific prayer. My prayer was different every day, for I genuinely believe in letting go and letting God. What followed was a guided meditation humming through my headphones. If I had enough time, I would do yoga on demand, which helped immeasurably. These practices were acutely therapeutic in easing the tension and anxiety I experienced. On the occasions I could not incorporate meditation into my morning, I noticed I cried a lot more and even felt physically sick. Praying and meditating didn't stop challenges from occurring; however, it made life considerably more manageable.

Several holidays came and went unmarked by grand celebrations, socializing, or traveling. Don's health was steadily declining, and any energy he had left after treatments were spent at home with the children and me, where he was most content. I was remaining faithful, as was Don. We both knew it might get worse before it got better.

Memorial Day arrived; I went into the kitchen to fix the children's lunch; when I returned to the bedroom with fruit for Don, he was struggling to breathe, I immediately called 911. Upon arrival at the hospital, he was placed on a ventilator. It would be the last day he would speak because of the tube in his throat. He was coherent for the first three days, eyes open, and able to answer my questions by blinking or squeezing my hand. On day four, he was no longer able to respond because his bodily functions were shutting down. On day six, with the children, immediate family, and I around his bed, Don slipped away from this world, tearing my heart into a billion pieces.

How could this be? I had been faithful; I prayed, I never ever doubted that he would get better.

The answers to these questions didn't come that day; I would quickly come to terms that even if you are faithful, sometimes God has a different plan.

That dreadful day and the weeks and months that followed are a forlorn blur of excruciating pain; I cried until my eyes were dry, I couldn't eat or sleep, and when I did manage to get something down, I became nauseous.

Thankfully, my wonderful mother and family attended to my children. The more I withdrew from everyone; the more people tried to console me. Even though I said I wanted to be left alone, I often felt relieved to have someone around.

I remember some days being pretty bad and others closer to unbearable. On one of those unbearable days, about three o'clock in the morning, I called my sister-friend and children's Godmother Linda Swanson. She listened to me cry and carry on for close to a half-hour. One of the things that bothered me most was feeling like I would never have the chance to share unsaid sentiments with Don.

After offering some encouraging words of prayer, Linda advised me to journal my thoughts, experiences past, current, future, and even write letters to Don. The next day I took her advice and purchased two beautiful leather embossed journals to begin my writing and soul searching. Late that night, while everyone else was sleeping, and I could not, I decided to break out my new journal and write Don a letter. On that one-page, I told him how much I missed him, how hard it was to make it without him, and right as I was signing the word love, I heard him call my name, "Kiko." I looked around and paused, not for long, I knew it was his voice. It sounded like he was in a tunnel, far away. He repeated, "Kiko, I love you," and I couldn't help but smile because at that moment I realized he was reading my letter.

From that day forward, I wrote in my journal consistently. I wrote down my every emotion, prayer, aspiration, dream, and most importantly, I wrote letters to Don. It was an introspective healing process and an outlet to release tears, anger, pain, and anguish. I can't say journaling magically erased my grief, but it was an immense aid in healing my soul.

The first three years without Don were the hardest, compelling me to throw myself into work, church, philanthropic endeavors, and my children. The exhausting schedule was intentional; of course, the more things on my agenda, the less time I focused on grief and depression. In the company of loved ones, social and work environments, I seemingly did well. It was the late-night hours, between 11pm and 5am, that I struggled the most. The realization that I was genuinely alone became more evident.

Yes, It was true that loving family and friends surrounded me. However, their presence could not diminish the undeniable void of a loving marriage and its fulfillment in the deep stillness of the night. It was during those late-night hours that the majority of my journaling took place. Journaling had become my way of coping, and by year four, it had opened my eyes and spirit to a thriving new life. My daily routine now included journaling, prayer, guided meditation, and yoga. I looked forward to every moment of those early morning sessions of self-love and preservation.

In year five, 2019, I learned to accept God's new purpose and plan for my life and let go of self-doubt and fear.

I learned to give myself permission to live, laugh and enjoy life on my terms. I stopped caring about people's time frames and opinions about where I should be in my life. It was a beautiful thing to wake up every morning and enjoy the sun shining on my face in the same place that used to be filled with pain. In embracing new beginnings with open enthusiasm, many amazing business and personal opportunities began to emerge.

Although I never gave much thought to having another serious relationship, I imagined that it would never be like the one I had with my late husband. Surely, I couldn't expect God to bless me a second time with a love like that when some have never found love at all. I was wrong. In that regard, I called upon my good friend, Gospel Legend and Pastor, Bishop Marvin Sapp, for counsel; he said to me, *"God does not ration blessings. His blessings are unlimited to the faithful. He will bless you abundantly above all that you can imagine."*

Several weeks later, right before Christmas, my mentor and cherished friend, Vivian Pickard, introduced me to my abundant blessing, Anthony L. Snoddy. Nine months later, Anthony became my loving husband, best friend, and soulmate! Once again, I am living, loving, and thriving beyond my wildest expectations! Together, my beloved King and I are passionately building a life rooted in love, happiness, health, family, and divine purpose.

By-the-way, it is true- God did not bless me with a love like the one I had; He blessed me with a love that is perfect for the woman I have become.

About Kiko Davis Snoddy

Kiko Davis Snoddy hails from Michigan and originally worked in real estate before becoming the trustee of the Donald Davis Living Trust. She is majority shareholder of the seventh largest African American owned bank in the United States. Mrs. Davis Snoddy is also the founder and president of the Don Davis Legacy Foundation, established in 2016, and Managing Director of Groovesville Productions & Publishing.

Currently Kiko Davis Snoddy is developing products for the beauty industry and producing a documentary while continuing to focus on empowering women.

She has received numerous accolades for her work including the Michigan Chronicle's Women of Excellence Award and the prestigious Ebony Magazine Power 100 Honor.

Connect with Kiko Davis Snoddy at kikodavis@gmail.com

WHEN LIFE STOPPED WHEN LIFE BEGAN

BY BARBRA GENTRY-PUGH

What If?

Wednesday, August 19, 2009, started as a normal day, but became a time in my life I will never forget. The circumstances will forever be a part of my memory! My life literally stopped, never to be the same again. My husband Robert was not breathing! I called his name, and he did not respond.

This cannot be! Oh God, what is going on? This is not real! I had just checked on him a few minutes earlier, and he seemed fine. I attempted to arouse him again, but he was unresponsive, with no palpable pulse. It was as if my heart fell to the bottom of my stomach! God, I do not understand what is going on?!

Being a retired Nurse with over 20 years of critical care experience, I went into emergency response mode. First, I called 911 and then immediately began C.P.R. (cardio-pulmonary resuscitation.) Sadly, I could not get Robert onto the floor to perform CPR effectively. Thank God it was not long before I heard the sirens of the ambulance!

Robert had been relatively healthy; he never spent one day in the hospital nor took prescription medication. He was a picture of health and rarely complained of any physical ailments. This was a mystery!

I remember kissing Robert and telling Diamond (his spoiled dog) goodbye. Then I left for work. As usual, we spoke three to four times throughout the day, but never once did he mention feeling ill.

Before leaving my office, I phoned Robert to tell him, I was on my way home. That is when he mentioned he may have been stung by a bee while working in the yard. I realized the potential seriousness of an allergic reaction and inquired if he was experiencing any signs or symptoms from the bee sting. He assured me that he was not having any symptoms. Yet, I advised him to go to the pharmacy close to our home and purchase some *Benadryl. He called me after taking the Benadryl and assured me he was okay. A while later, Robert called again, saying he felt a little dizzy and tired. I explained it was a common response to the medication and found no reason for concern. Robert had also worked in his mother's yard most of the day and was no-doubt overly exhausted.

When I arrived home, Robert was sitting in the lawn chair with Diamond, and said that he felt better, but sleepy. Yet, he continued to work for a while in the yard, until I convinced him to come inside. Instead of preparing for a shower, Robert decided to rest for a little while, and 15 minutes later, he was sleeping as I prepared dinner.

After preparing our meal, I went to see how he was doing and to ask him to take his shower. This was the last time I would speak to my husband.

When the paramedics arrived, they immediately intubated Robert to give him adequate respiratory ventilation and were able to get his heart beating. It was as though my world was in a tailspin and I was frozen in time. I'd never felt so helpless in my life!

In the emergency room, Robert was placed on life support and stabilization of his condition was in process. It seemed like hours before I could go to his bedside and when I did, it was evident that he was in critical condition. His cardiac monitor displayed abnormal heart rhythm indicative of heart muscle irritability and damage from lack of blood supply. However, I began to see the hand of God at work. Robert was transported to a hospital in Southfield, Michigan where I had worked as a contingent critical care nurse for nearly 20 years. This was the hand of God because I was acquainted with the Chief of Cardiology, Dr. David.

Dr. David took Robert to the Cath lab for a cardiac (heart) catheterization to evaluate the status of his heart.

Waiting for the results was grueling. In-between my mind fluctuating from the possible causes to the devastating effects, I was in constant prayer for a miracle. At one point, I even reasoned it was all a bad dream. Then, I began playing "The What If Game." What if I had insisted Robert call 911 and not wait for me to arrive home? What if I stayed with him and put off preparing dinner? What if I had just taken him to the hospital when I came home despite the fact he was not in any distress? What if?! What if?! What if?!

Fully understanding the sovereignty of God, I needed His comfort! I felt crushed like a knife was plunged into my chest! We had only shared seven short years of marriage together, and he vowed to be the best husband he could be. I was blessed to be the woman with whom he chose to make that commitment, and I wanted to grow old with him. This does not feel good, but God, "You" are in control.

After Robert's catheterization, he was transferred to the Cardiac Intensive Care Unit, under Dr. David's care. I met with Dr. David, who showed me the heart catheterization films that clearly revealed a massive heart attack. He also explained the recommended treatment plan for Robert's heart was to rest and heal. I now fully understood the graveness of the situation.

After hearing the news, I stayed at his bedside night and day. In doing so, I was forced to observe the irregular heartbeats and hear the constant alarms. At times it drove me out into the visitor's lounge for what relief could be found in the thinly cushioned chairs. I kept asking myself, "How did we get here?" The lyrics of a song we often sang in the choir came to mind "Hold To God's Unchanging Hand." A segment of one verse says, "Life is filled with swift transitions."

It is a mystery how Scripture and words of songs come to your mind in various situations. For me, life had taken a sudden turn, "made a swift transition."

The first night was exceedingly difficult. The constant alarms of Robert's heart monitor pierced my ears. The medication administered had no lasting effect. The love of my life had an abnormal rhythm, that said, I am leaving you for my eternal home. Our hearts will never beat together again as one.

After several days of being by my husband's side, God spoke to my heart and brought a verse of Scripture to me. 1 Thessalonians 5:18

"In everything give thanks; for this is the will of God in Christ Jesus for you." I said, "Oh, Lord, in this?" He said, "Yes." I did not feel any better when I read 1 Thessalonians 5:16-18.

"Be joyful always; pray continually; give thanks in all circumstances, for this is God's will for you in Christ Jesus."

Second guessing my actions was only causing Satan to distract and deceive me. God had decided that I had to trust, even though the pain was great. Some can only dream of love. But for a season, the gift was mine to have and to hold until death.

In the hours that followed, my prayers transitioned from petitions to humbly asking God for guidance and waiting for His direction. This gave me time to reflect on the Lord's faithfulness throughout my life.

Every time I needed Him to work things out, He came through. He is sovereign and could do anything!

The Neurologist came in to review the results of the EEG (electroencephalogram.) He did not have to explain in detail; the results were written all over his face. I stood there frozen, and he knew full-well I understood what was going on. I could not speak, tears rolled down my face, and he left the room.

In hindsight, I could see how God was beginning to prepare my heart. Numerous friends, family, and Pastors were calling and praying with me for a miracle. However, I surrendered in my finite mind to trust an infinite God who knows best even when I do not understand or like it.

I could hear the Word of God in Philippians 4:6-7;

"Don't worry about anything; instead, pray about everything. Tell God what you need and thank him for all he has done. Then you will experience God's peace, which exceeds anything we can understand. His peace will guard your hearts and minds as you live in Christ, Jesus."

I truly needed His peace because nothing was changing. Robert was slipping away, and I did not see how this was better for me. I know that Isaiah 55:8 says, "My thoughts are nothing like your thoughts," says the LORD. "And my ways are far beyond anything you could imagine." Intellectually, I understood that there are times when God says, "NO." But I would be lying if I said I understood God saying, "No," during Robert's illness. Especially when just a few years prior, He said, "Yes."

7 Years of Bliss

At the time, I was not interested in meeting anyone because I did not have time for a relationship. Yet, prior to a Sunday morning church service, our paths crossed for the first time. We greeted one another and I said to myself, "Wow, he is so handsome." I had no idea at the time who that handsome man would be in my life. As it turns out, Robert's sister-in-law, Lucille, and I sat by one another in the choir. She casually mentioned that he was single and then several months later suggested a plan. I was to invite her and her husband, Curtis, for a home-cooked meal. They, in turn, would invite Robert to come.

It was a set-up! "Me, cook?"

"Yes," she said, "cook!"

As you can see, I was not excited about the cooking idea. I did very little cooking. Besides, Sunday, after church, was my "me time." I would study, relax, and ready myself for the coming week.

"Robert has never been married," she coerced. "And it would be nice for him to meet a lady like you."

Well, the following Sunday after church, dinner became a reality. Yes, I cooked, and it felt uncomfortable not knowing what to expect. Robert appeared to be uncomfortable as well, but after we talked for an hour or so, things relaxed. The fellowship between us felt natural, and I must confess, enjoyable. He thanked me for dinner and said, "I would like to get to know you."

I responded, "It would be nice to get to know you as well."

Several weeks later, Robert called, and we had a great conversation. Soon, we began dating, but because of my busy schedule with work, school, and ministry, we talked on the phone more often than meeting in-person. Actual dates were reserved for Sundays. Yes, I cooked again!

After a rather lengthy courtship, on December 24, 2000, Robert officially asked me to be his wife and presented me with a large heart-shaped diamond. Two years later we were married on August 17, 2002. The seven years of marriage to Robert were some of the most wonderful years of my life. There was nothing within reason that I desired he did not attempt to provide. He supported me in everything I was involved in before and after our marriage. I loved him for many things, especially his generosity!

Yet, here we were, and God was saying, "No! I will Not heal Robert." I had to accept the reality that Robert was not coming home and that all our plans were halted in mid-stream. Right here is where I had to accept His "No" as a redirection of His plan for us according to His will.

The Lord took Robert home on the evening of **August 25, 2009**, along with everything I had become accustomed to. You see, although I had lived alone for many years, I had grown used to having the support and protection of a husband, and he was a great husband! This was the beginning of experiencing God as never before.

Emerging Triumphant

It was Saturday, two days after the funeral. The pain in my heart matched the status of a fresh open wound. I was alone and raw with pain. Our families had returned home, and the house was cold with silence. I felt lifeless, and there was so much to do. However, God was with me as I adjusted to the atmosphere of this new normal. The air was thinner at this level of cognizance causing me to gasp at times in the form of questions, Lord, why?" What is the meaning of all of this? "This is not what I signed up for!" Why God? I just do not get it!"

Now, before you begin to judge me for questioning God, let me assure you that I understand His sovereignty. However, on this day, I was coiled in my humanness and felt empty, alone, and abandoned. This was a layer of my healing process, and so was expressing my feelings directly to God.

As of today, eleven years after God ushered Robert into eternity. I have been left to trust God, live by faith, and allow His perfect plan to manifest in my life.

I am reminded of a particular Wednesday afternoon when I was drained and dreaded going home because of the long, lonely night ahead. I was okay at the office; I could close my door when I needed a moment to compose myself, but home was an empty, silent place. That evening I had the sensation of suffocating while walking down the hall to my bedroom. I stopped immediately feeling God's hand on my shoulder and cried out to the Lord. I simply said, "God, I need You!" I need to sleep, and I need your peace for the emotional pain and restlessness I feel in my heart.

From that moment forward, the Spirit of God began healing the pain in my heart. Thank You, Father! As of today, eleven years have passed since my husband passed away. During my restoration, I never pretended to be a super Christian. I simply recognized that grief is a natural response to pain and loss. It is an emotion that is mutual to the human experience, and we should respond biblically to the process! What you may be asking is, "How do I respond biblically to the process?"

For me, it was continually communicating with God, whether in prayer, shared emotions, and/or simply listening for God's guidance. Secondly: having the support of my Pastor, Christian friends, and family was invaluable. My Friends, Wilma Parham, and Yvette Rhodes took care of the program details, and my family flew in to be with me. Although it is wise to be in a grief counseling group/or session, I was blessed with support and did not feel alone. God is so good! These are examples of correct biblical responses that allow for a refreshing in your life.

Ultimately, as a widow, I had a choice to make. I could choose to be helpless and maintain an undesirable outlook or, I could view my loss from a new perspective and learn the lessons from the hard places of life. I chose the latter, knowing the lessons could shape the trajectory of my future. I am now able to embrace God's orchestration of beauty and love created just for me. This includes living a life of divine purpose and service to the Kingdom.

"The LORD says, "I will guide you along the best pathway for your life. I will advise you and watch over you."
Psalm 32:8 (NLT2)

Recovery Scriptures

**Psalm 23:4 "He is with us even in "the valley of the shadow of death."*

**Psalm 30:5, "Weeping may remain for a night, but rejoicing comes in the morning." Authors Commentary*

Mourning will not last forever! There is an end! The grieving process has a limit and a purpose. Praise God!

**Matthew 11:30, "For my yoke is easy to bear, and the burden I give you is light."*

**1 Peter 5:7, Cast all your anxiety on Him because He cares for you.*

**John 14:16, "And I will ask the Father, and he will give you another Advocate, who will never leave you."*

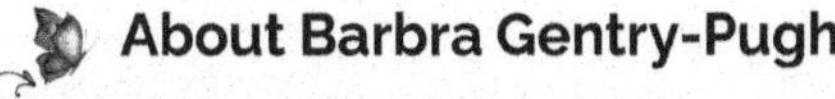

About Barbra Gentry-Pugh

Barbra Gentry-Pugh hails from the state of Texas but has lived in Michigan for many years. She holds several degrees and/or certifications in the following fields and/or occupations: Human Services, Christian Education, Nursing (Registered), International Life Coaching, and Biblical Counseling. She is a published author, Teacher and Public Speaker.

Mrs. Gentry-Pugh is CEO & Executive Director of Kairos-B-Enterprises, LLC, and founder and CEO of Heart Expressions Ministries International- a faith-based ministry devoted to reaching the heart of women one-beat at a time.

Her literary contributions include seven publications with *The Professional Woman Network* and an eighth anthology entitled, "*Gathering the Fragments That Nothing Will Be Lost,*" released in the fall of 2020. Mrs. Gentry-Pugh received a *PWN* International Literary Award for her debut release, *"Every Beat of My Heart."*

Connect with Barbra Gentry-Pugh at barbragp@gmail.com

TO LOVE AND LOVE AGAIN

BY LINDA HANNAH

To Love and Love Again

It was Monday, December 7, 2009, a morning like any other that found me getting ready for work. Howard was seated comfortably in the dining room, where both the TV and security monitors played simultaneously. His disability of Symptomatic Parkinson's' Disease challenged him physically; therefore, he employed a recliner whose seat lifted him almost to a standing position. Regardless of this challenge, he always got up and walked me to the door for a hug and kiss before I left. Sometimes I would say, "That's okay, Honey, stay seated." Seldomly would he remain seated.

This particular Monday morning, I suggested he remain seated; he said, "No, I'll walk you to the door." I responded, "It's okay," but he put his chair in motion to rise, and I didn't contest. Later that night and many days after, I was glad I didn't insist that he remain seated because it would be the very last time he stood to hug and kiss me goodbye.

Our middle child was at home with him. He would come over in the morning to stay with Howard during the day while I was at work. Sometime that afternoon, he called to say that his dad had fallen, and he couldn't pick him up. I immediately prepared to head home while dialing a friend of ours who could go over and help right away.

When I arrived home, Howard was lying in bed but less responsive than when he'd fallen before this incident. This time was different, and I called EMS, who transported him to the hospital. In the ER, the physician said that Howard had suffered a hemorrhagic stroke, otherwise referred to as brain bleeding. He had to have a procedure done immediately to relieve some of the pressure. Things were happening so fast, demanding that I answer questions, provide medications, and sign authorizations! Afterward, I was directed to a small waiting room where a doctor would come and talk with me.

Family members began arriving not long after the news, and we waited and prayed for the procedure to go well and for Howard to pull through. The waiting seemed so very long, but the prayer paid off-my husband's operation was a success but required him to remain in the ICU for a few weeks. Eventually, he was transferred to a long-term care facility, where he underwent rehabilitation for a few months. Through it all, I leaned on God and the peace He gave me daily. John. 14:27

There were times when Howard's condition fluctuated between bouts of lethargy and hints of improvement. Mostly, he remained unconscious with some semblance of a response to conversation and hand holding. I placed earbuds that streamed worship and praise music in his ears, knowing this would bless his spirit with peace and calm.

As I talked with Howard, I would share that the kids and I were doing fine, how much we loved him, and that people were praying for him continuously.

I knew it was important for me to tell Howard how I was doing so he wouldn't worry about my safety as I traveled back and forth. Having been a Detroit Police Officer, he was naturally protective; therefore, I assured him that I was careful and knew what to do when out and about. He had trained me well, and I could protect myself.

Periodically, I would think, "If I had driven home faster or told my son to call EMS immediately, it would have made a difference in the timing that he got medical attention." I felt that a few minutes sooner could have changed the outcome for the better. Falling wasn't totally foreign to us. You see, Howard would fall from time to time. He would make light of it, and we would laugh as we worked together at helping him get back up. That day I thought it would be as before, and he would be back on his feet as usual. This time it wasn't the same, and I was shocked.

Days and Weeks

Over the following weeks, the days and nights seemed like they blended together. God's word gave me strength – it was the anchor of my soul. I had to focus on something positive. That's why, even during this devastating situation, I told God that I was still grateful for each day we had together – for excellent health insurance and a wonderful and supportive family and friends. In addition to these factors, I had an awesome boss and wonderful colleagues.

There were two pastors from our church that would visit regularly, and it lifted my spirits whenever visitors came. The presence of others, their hugs, and warm smiles were so comforting.

Weeks turned into months, and I can remember one day feeling selfish. I actually said to myself that I wasn't the one suffering and if Howard wanted to go home to be with the Lord, who was I to fight that? Of course, I didn't want that; I wanted him to get better and recover.

On May 25, 2010, the day before my birthday, Howard peacefully went home to be with the Lord. It didn't feel real. After crying and comforting one another in the hospital family room, we began to leave. Then, almost immediately, there were time-sensitive decisions to make — like right then! Although a cliché, it is true that "time waits for no man." I was numb running on autopilot while answering questions and needing to ask a few of my own.

The following day was my birthday, but so was a scheduled trip to the funeral home to make arrangements for Howard. I was just going through the motions of trying to get things done when my brother and his wife called from Tampa. They told me not to make his arrangements on my birthday, that it could wait a day. Instead, they sent me to a spa to relax and be personally cared for. I brought a girlfriend along for company and comfort, and that's what I did on my birthday. I was so glad they suggested that I delay making arrangements.

Howard and I would have been celebrating 30 years of marriage come that September 6. Our last child living at home had bought a house and moved four months before Howard became ill. We were looking forward to moving ourselves and doing some traveling. But this one day would forever change the course of our lives.

After five months of being at the hospital every day, suddenly, all that activity came to a halt. My days and nights slowed down immensely, leaving me with a need to be occupied. Although I had previously made hats and wanted to be busy doing something, I didn't have the motivation. I decided to enroll, along with my mother, in a year-long Laypersons' Bible program. I felt it would be a positive diversion for me having to learn, study and apply myself.

Subconscious Habit

If not eating dinner at my parents, with my daughter, or at a friend's house, I ate out or carried out. One evening I became aware that whenever I entered a restaurant, and was asked, "How many?" I would respond, "Only one," or "Just one." It wasn't really the words that gave me pause, but my tone, which conveyed -"It's only me." After that, I made an intentional decision to speak in my usual tone as I proceeded.

Emotional Trigger

One of my co-workers was getting married in 2011. I decided to go on my lunch hour to buy their gift from the store, "*Things Remembered.*" I went on their web-site ahead of time to get an idea of what I wanted to buy. Once there, I looked at a couple of other items, made a purchase, and wrote down the inscription.

The sales lady said it would be ready in about 20 minutes. I decided to get something from the food court while I waited to take back to work.

Upon exiting the store, for no apparent reason, I began feeling very emotional. Each step I took felt heavy as I tried to pull myself together. I just wanted to sit down and let it out, but I knew I couldn't. I silently prayed, "God, you've gotta help me get to the food court and sit down." I didn't want to break down crying in the middle of the mall — that would involve strangers and possibly security trying to assist me, and I wanted to avoid any attention. Thankfully, I made it to a seat that shrouded my presence, keeping my delicate condition discreet. Calming, I softly prayed for strength, knowing I had to go back to *"Things Remembered."*

After sitting a while, I felt strengthened and returned to the store to pick up the gift with no problem. I visited that store again a year or two later and thankfully didn't relive that experience. Daily, I depended on my relationship with the Lord to get me through challenging days, and He never failed. He is all comforting! 2 Corinthians 1:3 reads —

I will strengthen you; I will also help you,
I will also uphold you with My righteous right hand. (ESV)

The Firsts

There can be some sensitivities to approaching what I call "first time" days, such as holidays, birthdays, anniversaries, and the day of a loved-ones passing, especially if it was the day before your birthday. Be aware of those upcoming days and plan to go someplace, be with a friend or take a trip – be intentional about how you will spend those days. If you don't want to go anywhere and rather be alone, that's okay. But when alone, reflect on pleasant memories that you have.

- Holidays: This was the first Christmas Eve at my parent's house without Howard. I definitely felt a void, although I was among my wonderful, loving family. On Christmas, I spent most of the day with my daughter, son-in-law, and twenty-three-month-old grandson, who was a delight to be around! Later, we went out to dinner. On New Year's Eve, my parents were invited to a friend's event and asked me to come along. I'm glad that I went; being with my Mom that evening was quite enjoyable.

- Invitations: Accept invitations as gestures of love – even when you feel as if you cannot stop or take a break. A very dear friend of mine insisted that I take a one-day break away from the rehabilitation center to spend the day and night at her place while her husband and children were away. She prepared my favorite meal and ran me a tub of hot water in their Jacuzzi surrounded by lit candles. It was like I was at a spa retreat. This peaceful and pleasant getaway blessed my soul!

- Living On: In January of 2012, I made plans to meet up with a friend and former co-worker to visit her church. I had been a member of my church for 23 years, but I kept getting a sense to visit my friend's church. As I entered the foyer on my first visit, I passed their information/resource center. My eyes fell upon a card rack, and one, in particular, got my attention – it read, "LIVING ON – A Support Group for Those Who Have Lost a Spouse." I picked it up and put it in my purse. Later I found out that they met quarterly; I couldn't make it to the March session but planned to attend the meeting in June. When I went, I was greeted with a warm, loving smile from Pastor Shirley McClelland. She asked how I was doing and if there was anything she could pray with me about. She shared the mission of the ministry and availed herself to be a listening ear. She told me that another woman named Theresa led the ministry with her, and she was now engaged to be married next year. I quickly said, "Well, that's nice for her," followed by, "I won't be getting married again."

One Day in 2012

One beautiful summer afternoon in 2012, I was driving home from work, and as I looked upward at the sky out of my mouth came, "Lord, I want to love and be loved again." Suddenly I felt a sense of excitement, and I had peace. It didn't mean that I would ever forget about my life with Howard; I never could.

"Your spouse is a part of your life's fabric, woven into your soul by years of living and loving."

Lost and Found: Finding Self-Reliance After the Loss of a Spouse, by P. Mark Accettura and Steven J. Case.

I also believed deeply that Howard prayed for God to bring along another husband – he was that type of man – one who would want a continued love and covering for me. When I shared my declaration with my friend Theresa, she said it sounded like I was opening my heart up to love again. A month or so later, she mentioned online dating, and I quickly put the brakes on that comment with, "No way! I'm protective, private, and not trying it!" I told her I wanted to continue wearing my wedding ring so that no one even approached me. She didn't bring it up again. But, in February of 2013, it came to my heart to try online dating. When I told Theresa, I added, "I'm trying this for six months, and if I do not meet anyone, that's a wrap!"

I had been happily married for 30 years and had three great children; I would be good. I did, however, meet several nice gentlemen, but not one of them was for me. I wasn't motivated to keep looking, so I deactivated my profile to take a break from it.

Staying Busy

I made it a point to stay very busy, at one point deciding to get back into roller skating – something I loved doing since I was nine years old. I went a few times and really enjoyed it, so I bought new skates and began going weekly. It was a healthy and active outlet for me - something I looked forward to.

My schedule after work was:

Monday - Golf Lessons
Tuesday - Ballroom Lessons
Wednesday - Church Usher
Friday - Golf League (don't be impressed!)
Saturday - Roller Skating

I felt it was important for me to stay active, and one of my favorite things to do was being a greeter at church. I did this every Wednesday for mid-week service and twice a month on Sundays. That led to an invitation to usher, which I also enjoyed. Being able to greet people as they entered the church with a smile, handshake, or hug was my way of ministering love. One never knows what a person is dealing with, and I believed that a smile could help to soothe away some stress as they came in. I wanted the love of God to smile through me and touch hearts.

Six-month Mark

In August 2013, I reactivated my online dating profile, and that's when Keith and I met! He had also deactivated his online account. So, when we were led to reactive our accounts simultaneously, that's when we saw each other!

Early on in getting to know one another, I had a feeling in my heart that Keith was "the one" for me. I prayed for God's wisdom and insight about this. I then told my brother, sisters, Mom, and kids about him. Lastly, Keith passed the grandson and the dog test! I also realized that I had met Keith right in the middle of August, six months from when I began online dating and the cut-off period I gave myself if things didn't work out.

God knew I wouldn't renege on the cut-off date, so we had to meet by then. We began courtship classes a few weeks later and married on July 19, 2014!

Where, Who, What

Below are some things that I considered as time moved along, and you may want to do the same one day:

- What did you enjoy doing years ago that you can begin to do or to learn again?

- Who can you encourage? There is always someone that we can help, even when we are hurting. It takes us off of our mind, which is a good thing, and allows the Lord to direct us to where we can be a blessing.

- Where can you volunteer?

- What family or friend can you visit in another state or country that can be a welcomed change of scenery?

My Source of Strength

My resilience through being widowed came from my relationship with the Lord. For it is through Him that I live, move, and have my being. He was my source of strength and comfort – daily. And He used so many people in my life, which I called God Appointments or Destiny Intersections, to help me in various ways. The following experiences depict just two examples of God's appointed people in my life.

I became a landlord of the home Howard and I lived in for 30 years because I leased a condo only weeks before

Howard's passing. I did this to be closer to him, not knowing he would be gone before I relocated. I now needed a property manager and shared my plight with my nail technician. Coincidentally, her cousin was in this line of work, and she gave me the contact information. This woman proved to be INCREDIBLE at managing the property!! She was a person of her word and handled matters that popped up here and there on every turn. I never had to be concerned that she wouldn't follow through on what she said. That gave me peace and was a blessing!

On one occasion, there was a plumbing issue occurring at the house while I was at the hospital, and it had gotten worse. I was sharing with a colleague how I had to find someone to take a look. She told someone who was the CEO of a company of highly skilled journeymen. He, in turn, sent someone to the house to assess and fix the problem. I attempted to pay and was told, "We are not to accept any payment from you and would get in trouble if we did."

These are just a couple of ways that God moved upon people in my world. Stay encouraged because God knows all about you in every way, and He will at times answer prayers before you hardly speak them. Just as a parent loves surprising their children, I believe God, who is the Ultimate Parent, would not do any less for His children.

"He does exceedingly and abundantly more than we can ask or think." Ephesian 3:20 (NKJV), and all "His plans for us are good," Jeremiah 29:11. (NIV).

Moving Forward

In the process of moving forward, focus on your heart recovering. You can facilitate restoration by spending time talking with God, reading a book about dealing with the loss of a loved one, and through counseling or grief support. God is all comforting.

"Blessed be the God and Father of our Lord Jesus Christ, the Father of mercies and God of all comfort."
2 Corinthians 1:3 (ESV).

Adjusting to being single again and dealing with matters by yourself is different for everyone. Remember, people do want to be a blessing to you, so ask for help. Rearranging things in your world might be needed at different points, such as relocating or a career move. Seek counsel or family help for guidance, and don't make any major decisions soon after such a big loss. You will develop as you walk this new path discovering what's next, one step at a time. There is no hurry to do anything different or new as you move forward.

Focus

On

Resting

While

Adjusting

Recovering

Developing

Let me close by saying that you will move forward each day at your own pace. Take one day at a time while looking reasonably ahead to plan. However, do not stress yourself out with too many expectations of where you think you should be on this journey or how long it should take. There is life and love after "death do us part" in the earth. You have a heavenly Father who created love, and that love never ceases to be with you.

About Linda Hannah

Detroit native, Linda Hannah is a senior commercial contract analyst in the utility industry and a graduate of the University of Michigan-Dearborn. She took lessons at Mertize Millinery in Detroit and then started a hat business. For more than 20 years she and her late husband custom designed many one-of-a-kind pieces for avid hat wearers and several boutiques, while teaching the craft at a local fabric store and workshops for an American Sewing Guild conference.

She is also founder of *Hat Moments* and speaks about the history of hats worn throughout the decades.

Linda is the mother of three, and grandmother of two. She found new love with her husband, Keith, and they reside in Farmington Hills, Michigan. Linda enjoys roller skating, traveling and spending time with family and friends.

Connect with Linda Hannah at linda@hatmoments.com

BRIGHTER DAYS AHEAD

BY DORIS HANNAH TURNER

Brighter Days Ahead

It was Saturday, July 27th, 2019, at 6:03 a.m. I just lost my husband and best friend of 44 years, eighteen hours, and three seconds. As I took stock of my life, I wondered where had all the years gone. We never really realize how time has slipped away until that special person in our life is no longer with us.

My husband and I raised three beautiful, talented children together and have been blessed with five grandchildren and one great-grandchild. I never lived by myself before; I moved directly out of my parents' home and in with my husband. But from now on, I would be responsible for every decision I make. No more, "Honey, everything is going to be alright." I had to figure life out and move on.

When Michael died, my income was cut in half. Funny how I was always concerned about how he would handle everything if something happened to me. I never thought about what I would do if something happened to him.

In June of 2017, we took a road trip south to visit family and friends. Accompanying us was our daughter Phyllis, two of our youngest grandchildren, Codee and Caree, and our god-daughter Pearl. A few days before our return to Michigan, Michael noticed that he had a lot of swelling in his legs. My cousin Joyce, who used to be a nurse, took his blood pressure, and found it to be quite elevated.

All of us were so concerned about Michael that we dropped everything off at the house when we returned to Michigan and proceeded to John D. Dingell, V.A. Medical Center, in Detroit. Michael was admitted, and they performed many tests. After days and days of testing, one doctor discovered a rare blood disorder called A.L. Amyloidosis. Over time, this blood disorder causes a person's internal organs to shut down.

In 1988, Michael had Ulcerative Colitis, then Prostate Cancer in 2010, but emerged cancer-free after treatment. Now, we were dealing with this, and there was no way to gauge the rough road ahead. No matter- I told myself throughout the years that I would make it in life no matter what comes my way. This was my version of a positive attitude. Michael once shared that he drew his strength from me because of my positive attitude. My mantra was, "Honey, it could be worse."

I challenge every reader to remember my mantra when you're going through life's challenges start counting your blessing. I promise you they will outweigh your problems. Only need I had given my heart to Jesus when I was nineteen years old.

If ever there was a time to exercise my Christian faith, it was now.

I tried not to lose myself in the midst of being a mother and a wife- This was challenging for me because it seemed as if I never had time for myself. However, Michael was very protective of me and always supported my ideals; even my alter ego-personality, Lady Dean- He allowed me to grow and venture out in life.

Off-topic, my mother was great when it came to teaching us lessons about life. I received more lashings than any of my other four siblings, making me very familiar with the tree branches on Oakley Street. Everyone called my childhood neighborhood the Boondocks, which is located in the small town of Mount Clemens, Michigan. We learned how to make and save money, cook, clean, and wash clothes with an old-fashioned washing machine- the kind that had a wringer. We had to hang the clothes outside on the clothesline. This made me feel as if I were raised up in the south, but it was the 70's, and we were in the North.

I'm sharing all of this to let you know that I felt like I was raised to be a housewife, and never during my upbringing did I realize that I could be more than that.

My husband loved me through many of my life transitions, such as my weight fluctuation, losing my hair, and various other changes- he accepted me for who I was. I knew that he loved me second after God. My dear friends, I hope everyone can experience that kind of love in their life one day.

Before we go any further, I can tell you that, no, life was not always peaches and cream, but we worked through challenges with God as our head.

I know some of you are businesswomen, and times have changed drastically, but I am sure that there are still women out there who do not have credit in their name or have a decent credit score. If your credit score is not up to par, then fix it, A.S.A.P., you never know when you might need it.

Back to the story about dealing with Amyloidosis; my husband and I battled with this illness for two years. Before the diagnosis, we were caregivers for his father, who passed away in April 2014, and for his mother, whom he lost in August 2015.

Yes! You are right; life just doesn't seem fair. Michael has cared for so many people; he was a man of God and did everything he was supposed to. We were in our prime, and I wanted us to spend a long healthy life together. Unfortunately, there is no cure for this illness, leaving you to wonder, what will become of our lives? One thing we must realize is that "Bad Things Happen to Christians Too."

This disease most definitely changed our lives with numerous visits to hospitals, Chemotologists, Nephrologist, and Cardiologists. There were also the added treatments of dialysis, blood transfusions, and dental care. The list goes on and on. Sometimes we were at doctors' appointments five times a week.

Nevertheless, I was right by my husband's side, giving him all the love, emotional and physical support I could provide. I loved him with all my heart and would do anything to make his life as easy as possible.

In June of 2019, I noticed that Michael's health was declining. He had scars all over his back as if someone took a whip to him. His eyes were yellow, and his appetite had decreased. He didn't seem steady enough to drive, so I began driving him around like I did at the beginning of his illness. When my nephew David and our niece, Denise, came for a visit from Arizona, I asked Denise, a registered nurse, about my concerns. She gave me some wise advice that I will never forget. She said, "Cherish the time that you have with him." I did just that even more than ever. I appreciated her being honest with me, it reconfirmed my thoughts, but I still didn't realize that his time was drawing nigh probably because I was always so busy and didn't have time to think about it.

We were scheduled to attend a family reunion in Rochester, New York, the second weekend in July. As Michael struggled to get in and out of the car, he said, "This will probably be my last time going on a trip." I responded to him. "I know, honey, I know."

We made it through the weekend, and on Tuesday, he had an appointment with his primary care physician. I explained everything to her just as I had explained to his doctor in the dialysis department. I could feel in my heart and innermost being that something wasn't right. The doctor ordered tests that Tuesday, July 16th. The next morning, she told him to go straight to emergency after dialysis. They performed a biopsy of his liver.

It was now Wednesday, July 24th. I got up early to prepare some soup for Michael when I realized I had so much extra that I needed to give some away. I reached the Johnson sisters and delivered the extra soup to them on the way to the hospital. En route, I received a call from Michael's Chemotologists. She asked me to come to her office before I go to see my husband. My niece Alesada was already in the area and met me at the hospital. She went to give Michael his soup while I went to see his doctor. There was that feeling in the pit of my stomach, again indicating that the news would not be good. I was told that Michael had Cholangiocarcinoma, in short, bile duct cancer and that this type of cancer can take you out faster than pancreatic cancer, which is what his sister, Linda, died from in 2014. I recall her saying, "I didn't see this coming."

I can't remember what I thought initially, but I knew I had to be strong until after visiting Michael. Telling him now was out of the question because I hadn't processed the news myself. I even asked the doctor to tell my children because I could not. The three of them came quickly-Michael Jr., Samuel, Phyllis, our niece Alesada and goddaughter, Pearl. When the doctor delivered the results to them, I could see their hearts drop in despair. She concluded by saying there was nothing they could do, and he probably had three months to live.

These are words no one wants to hear, but through their aftermath, I kept assuring myself that I could handle this-that God would help me through it. I told the children that mama can't fix this one and that they had to find strength themselves.

Michael was in dialysis, and I had to pick him up because he couldn't take a full treatment. Everyone who couldn't keep a straight face I told them to exit the room. A few left and the rest stayed.

It was Thursday morning, July 25th. All the girls, including our great-niece Zharia, came with me because the doctor was meeting me in Michael's room at 7:30 a.m. I told them to adjourn in the waiting room until the doctor finished talking to us. When I entered the room, the doctor wasn't there yet. Tears flowed down my cheeks, and I said to him, "Honey, I have to tell you something. I have been married to you for 44 years, and I can't let the doctor tell you something that I know."

I told him everything the doctor shared with me and the children. The doctor walked in and shared the same information and answered any questions he had for her.

The bottom line was, "nothing could be done." He told us that he wanted to go home and receive hospice care. Before the doctor left the room, she said to us, "You two are the strongest people that I have ever known," and that she admired our faith in God. It was after she left the room we embraced each other and told one another how much we loved each other. I stayed until the evening, then Michael Jr. spent most of the night with him while I went to our grandson's last soccer game.

I must reiterate, I did not realize that time was drawing nigh. That evening I called three people: Our pastor, David Lunn, and two of his fireman buddies, L. Taylor, and H. Kennedy, who had a ministry in visiting the sick.

Kennedy said he would be there the next morning, which was Friday. When he arrived, he gave Michael communion to ensure that he was in right standing with God. Afterward, we stood in the hospital hallway, and Kennedy asked me how I felt about Michael going home to be with the Lord? I said I'm okay with it because I don't want him to suffer.

He said, "You have to tell him how you feel."

I said, "I think he knows."

Kennedy then looked at me and responded, "Doris, you have to tell him."

I finally agreed.

Then he kindly asked before he departed, was there anything else he could do? Sadly, there was nothing else anyone could do. I called the social worker to get the wheels turning to bring Michael home that day. He needed the comfort of his own home that he loved so much. It was our retirement home. We had only been there for five years. I called all the children, my daughter-in-love, Lori, and son-in-love, Charo. Lori got to the house first, informing me that all the equipment had arrived. When Michael went into the hospital on July 18th, he was able to walk. On Thursday, before he went home, he used the walker a little. When he was released on Friday, he could get in the car with a bit of assistance. On the way home, he could barely keep his eyes open. We stopped by the garden we worked so hard on to see it from the car, and I picked a few veggies for him.

Michael's prayers had always been, "Lord, keep me in my right mind and let me be able to take care of myself. Only God knows the hour, the minute, and the second of our life on this earth."

Hospice was scheduled for Saturday morning, July 27th. When we arrived, the boys had to literally carry their father into the house. Michael was able to recognize and account for everyone that he wanted to see. I knew he did not like everyone having to wait on him, and I believe in my heart that he decided right then and there to ask God to take him home. He hadn't seen Codee and Caree for a while and was happy to see them. After the excitement of having him home began to wane everyone went home except our daughter Phyllis, who always found a reason to stick close by our side. Michael Jr. returned later that night and spent time reflecting on his father's life with an interview that shed light on how he felt about each of us.

I think it's a beautiful thing to have the memories or your parent's words recorded. Michael Jr. left around 4:00 a.m., and that's when I came down to be with Michael Sr. He asked me for half of his pain pill- he never complained about pain. He wanted to be coherent, and in his right mind, so he was always careful about taking medication. I had to pull the hassock closer to Michael because I couldn't hear anything he was saying. I wanted to lay down beside him so badly, but I couldn't because there wasn't enough room. We started talking about fear, and I asked him, was he afraid of anything? He said no.

He asked me the same question, and I said, only if he was. I asked was he concerned about the children and me? He said yes. I assured him that we would be okay, and if he wanted to go home, it was okay and, I would be okay. He asked me for the other half of his pain medication, and I gave it to him. He patted his chest for me to lay my head there. Michael said to me; I don't know why I just can't get comfortable. About ten minutes later, he started to gurgle, but I heard of it as a death raddle. Fluids began coming from his mouth. I called Phyllis to come down. I laid my hands on him and called out to God and began to pray in the spirit. I asked God to take him home if his work was finished here and receive his son in the name of Jesus....and it was finished. Through faith, I know that death is the door to heaven.

As we carefully planned the home-going celebration for my husband. I began to realize that he was a hero not only to me but to many others. I also started to evaluate myself and my relationship with God. I knew I had a journey ahead of me and that I needed God more than ever. I wanted His will for my life and not mine.

When I was fourteen years old, my oldest sister Anna had a friend named Marilyn; she had a few brothers Herman and Anderson. Anna and Herman were sweet on each other, and the three of them tried to get Anderson and me together. I don't remember all the details, but Anderson does, and this is the story through his eyes.

He said his brother had been coaching him about girls because he was timid. One day they decided to invite me over and put music on so we could dance in his mother's kitchen. When the music went off, he ran upstairs because he didn't know what to do next. Well, that was the end of that! Afterward, I remember seeing Anderson only at the school snack bar to get cherry pies where I was working. I was interested in older guys anyway.

Let's fast forward. It was a few years ago when I saw Anderson on Facebook, and we connected as friends. I was excited to reconnect with someone from high school. I called him on messenger, and we talked about what we have been doing for the past 40 years.

Michael was sitting beside me, and he asked me, "Who is that?" I said just someone I knew in high school.

I often said, if something happened to my husband, I would be happy with my children and grandchildren. I miss my husband more than anything, and if I could choose, I would choose for him to be here with me with no sickness. Yet, I realized that I needed a friend to confide in. My children had their own lives, and I did not want to be a burden to them. One day during my devotion, I was talking to God about how I felt. I told Him that I wanted a friend in my life. I asked God to choose for me with two specific things in mind.

1. Someone who truly loved Him (God) because I knew if that person would be loyal to God, they could be true to me.
2. Someone that could take care of themselves financially. I felt my husband looked out for me before and after his death. I was not going to let someone come and mess things up in my life.

When Anderson found out on Facebook that I lost my husband, he contacted me on messenger. He wanted to know if there was anything he could do for me. I assured him that I was fine. After my conversation with God, Anderson came across my mind a few times. I tried not to pay any attention because I needed to be sure it was God and not me feeling alone. — Although Anderson did send me motivational scriptures daily.

One thing about me is that I am very outspoken; you don't have to guess what's on my mind. So, I asked Anderson why he was so attentive to me; was it about sex? He assured me that it wasn't, and he wanted to be there for me. I found out later that he said he had to move fast because I was a good catch.

One day, I was at the apple orchard with my family and decided to leave them and go to the store. While I was walking, tears began to stream down my face. I was missing Michael more than ever when my phone rang; it was Anderson. I told him I couldn't talk and would call him back that evening. After talking to him, I felt connected. He wanted to see me, but I said after I come back from South Africa, which was about two weeks away. Well, I finally agreed to see him before I left. We met at his home, and when he opened the door for me, he looked very anxious. What I didn't expect when we hugged was a kiss as well. I asked him not to do that again. He thought I wouldn't continue to see him and said he didn't want to do anything to mess up.

While I was in South Africa, we saw each other every night on the What's App. While I had many sleepless nights, it was morning in Michigan for him.

We poured ourselves out to each other, his hurt, pain, and how he made so many mistakes in life. I shared about my life with Michael. One thing he said to me is that "I just want a little bit of what Michael had, and that was happiness. When I came home in November, It was like God turned a light bulb on in my heart. I was as anxious to see him as he was to see me, and that, my dear friends, is when I fell in love with Anderson. He encourages me in everything I do. He helped make decisions about my book of poetry, "An African Rock" He encouraged me in whatever else that I am interested in doing. He loved the fact that I was confident in who I am and especially being bald. Who would have known that the dance in the kitchen with a shy boy and a fast girl would find each other after 48 years to be a match? Whatever God has for me, my heart is open, whether it's marriage or a friend for life. He is a handsome, intelligent, thoughtful, funny, sweet, gentle, loving, and kind Christian man. To be loved twice in a lifetime is a beautiful gift from God.

Brighter Days Ahead

Candy apples, hayrides in Ypsilanti
It was my first time getting a call from you.

Teary-eyed walking through the space of land Wondering
when would my eyes dry.

Joy, laughter, and sharing my memories of him with you
Eases the pain and helps me walkthrough
The Journey of Life that seemed so empty. Words of
wisdom that helps me float through.

Sunshine and brighter days have broken through. Thank you, God, for ordering my path in that direction To help me along the way.

Though my heart shall never forget the love that I shared, It helped me put my life in perspective
As I travel, dear Lord, this journey of life with you.

By Doris D. Hannah Turner

Things To Remember

- Keep a Journal
- Don't be upset with God
- Make sure your life is in order
- Take good care of yourself
- Realize that you are not alone
- Thank God for everything
- Talk to him about everything
- Stay around positive people
- When you get up in the morning, find a way to be a blessing to someone else
- Remember your circle in life is not complete
- Set goals for yourself
- Do something that you never had a chance to do

About Doris Hannah Turner

Doris Dean Hannah Turner hails from Michigan and earned a certificate in Ministry from the California School of Ministry and later earned her certification in the rules of etiquette behavior from "*The Etiquette Institute*" in St. Louis, Missouri.

Her credits include being co-founders of "***Lady Butteries,***" a mentorship program, "***Delectable Soups***" especially prepared by Doris, and her portrayal of a comedic personality, *Lady Dean.*

Doris' creates and designs afro-centric dolls and penned her first book, "*An African Rock: Sacred Poems of Love, Loss, Legacy, and Life.*"

Doris was immensely overjoyed with 44 years of partnership, love, and devotion with her husband Michael until his passing on July 27th, 2019. Yet, Doris stands victorious through each milestone knowing Jesus Christ has always been her comforter and guide.

Connect with Doris Hannah Turner at turnerdd62@gmail.com

HONOR HIM
AND him
BY LIVING YOUR LIFE

BY LACHARMINE (L.A.) JEFFERSON

Death Doesn't Come as Expected Even When It's Expected

I was released from the scene of the fire a little after midnight, less than an hour after the ambulance left with my husband, Kevin. My sister was with my two children and me. I'd called her when it became clear that this fire wasn't going to be one of the well-kept secrets of me and Kevin's marriage. I needed support that only my family could provide.

On the short drive to the hospital, I was consumed by a range of emotions vacillating between fear, sadness, disbelief, and anger. There was no doubt in my mind that Kevin had caused the fire- It didn't matter that I went so far as to post signs around the house on the danger of smoking while using oxygen, or how much I complained, he wouldn't stop doing it!

"You're risking everyone else's life for the pleasure of your addiction!" I shouted during an argument in 2016.

His response knocked the wind out of me. "Where is your faith? Do you think God is going to let anything happen to you because of me?" He asked sincerely.

For as long as I knew Kevin, ten years—5 dating and five married—he'd lived as though the rules didn't apply to him. I'd witnessed God spare him from the consequences that his actions were so deserving of. When he should've been kicked out of hotels for continually breaking the "no smoking" policy, he wasn't. He'd made nice with the hotel housekeeping staff, and they overlooked it. When he should have lost his job or been suspended for mismanaging his company credit card records, he wasn't. Instead, he was able to retire on a medical disability, with full benefits, before he got in really hot water.

On Sunday, December 17, 2017, God had a different plan for Kevin.

It had been a typical weekend for us. On Friday, the 15th, we had an awesome time together at Kevin's sister's 50th surprise birthday party, then a huge fight Saturday morning about something insignificant, and slowly began making up on Sunday. By late evening, we were on speaking terms when my daughter, LaTya, arrived and decided to sleep at home. She slept in the bedroom upstairs. My 13-year-old son, Nate, was in the other room, along with our two dogs, Tristen, and Pepper.

Around 10:30 p.m., I fell asleep on the couch while watching a Christmas movie on the Hallmark channel. Kevin was tucked away in the downstairs bathroom, smoking, and making beats on his music machine. I closed my eyes, fully aware that he was smoking while using the supplemental oxygen required for his interstitial lung disease.

I also knew that he was unafraid of all the things I'd warned him about since he'd been diagnosed in 2015. I can't be sure if I'd begun to trust that Kevin wouldn't let anything happen to me or if my faith rested in God.

Not even an hour after I'd fallen into as comfortable a sleep as one can on the couch, the fire alarm jolted me awake! I leaped from the couch, made a dash for the kitchen a few feet away, and met Kevin's eyes at the point of a torch-like flame shooting from the oxygen cord. That cord was connected to one of the three 1000 lb. liquid oxygen tanks sitting in our dining room.

Our house didn't explode as rumored but standing outside watching flames escape through my living room window, reminded me of what I had feared for quite some time. I'd call 911 with shaky fingers just before getting all of us, except the dogs, out of the house. Fire Station #2 was right around the corner, and I had no doubts that they'd be there soon enough to rescue our dogs and salvage the house. After all, we'd just moved in two months earlier.

It didn't go as I'd hoped. The firemen, likely cautious about entering a burning house with oxygen tanks inside, didn't rush to get my dogs out. They both perished, releasing my first set of tears that night. When I arrived at the nearby hospital where the ambulance took Kevin, I was informed that he was on life support. That spawned the second set of tears.

"Life support?" I repeated in disbelief- This couldn't be. Kevin looked just fine when they lifted him from the porch and placed him on the stretcher. All they needed to do was connect him to an oxygen supply, and he should have been fine. But, apparently, my husband had been without supplemental oxygen longer than I realized. He'd gone into cardiac arrest right there on the porch as we waited for help to arrive. I would later learn that the EMT performed CPR on Kevin for 45 minutes to get a pulse from him.

Immediately I was saddled with guilt. Should I have seen that Kevin wasn't okay? Did he try to give me a signal that I missed? If I weren't preoccupied with the dogs trapped in the upstairs bedroom, maybe I would have noticed he was in distress.

Honestly, I was just so damn used to Kevin coming out victorious no matter what mess he'd gotten himself into that I didn't see this coming out any differently! In fact, driving to the hospital, I was practicing how I would address him when I walked into his room. Naturally, I couldn't begin with, "Kevin, what the hell happened?" I would have to start with showing genuine concern about his health.

"Are you alright, honey?" "How are you feeling?"

But I desperately wanted to know what the hell started that fire.

Unfortunately, it wasn't in God's plan for me to ask any questions that day or any other. Kevin passed away a few hours later, surrounded by family. I'd called his oldest daughter, and the news spread like wildfire through the family pipeline. Within no time at all, the family that I wished had been there for us over the past two years of Kevin's illness were there when he breathed his last breath.

That was not the death that Kevin and I anticipated.

Since the day of his diagnosis with interstitial lung disease, Kevin began preparing me for losing him. The scarring on his lungs caused by the disease led to obstruction of his oxygen supply. The day of his diagnosis, he was prescribed one of the highest doses of 24/7 supplemental oxygen authorized. But, as the disease rapidly progressed, the amount was barely enough. Both of us surmised that he would either pass away during his sleep- a fear that created a severe case of insomnia for him, or he'd be admitted to the hospital, connected to machines, and just drift off quietly into death.

I didn't expect the mix of emotions that followed. Sure, there was shock, devastation, and sadness- that was expected. I'd not only lost my husband but my new home, including most of our possessions and my two dogs. And if not for the quick thinking of my thirteen-year-old son, Nate, I could have lost my daughter. I didn't realize until after the fire that the room she'd been sleeping in received most of the smoke; it was directly above the downstairs bathroom where the fire started. Nate had run upstairs to wake her up while Kevin and I were trying to smolder the fire blowing out of the oxygen cord. As an asthmatic, things could have ended badly for her. BUT GOD!

Still, the possibility of her being harmed enraged me! Anger that my daughter, my son, and myself were at risk because Kevin refused to stop smoking. Anger that I'd accepted his smoking from the start of our relationship. Anger that I could never express my feelings to him or get an explanation about what happened that night. Anger that I felt obligated, as the grieving widow and loving wife, to protect his reputation—in death as I had in life—and keep what I knew to be the truth from my family and his.

Then, I felt guilty for being angry on the way to the hospital when I should have been concerned. Guilty over the thought that there was something I didn't do to save my husband's life. Guilty that I hadn't been a better caregiver for him and stored some emergency oxygen tanks in the car or something. The thought that I might have failed him when he needed me most was crushing!

Death saved Kevin from the aftermath of the fire. I was left to pick up the pieces of the mess he caused. After being asked to repeat the events that led up to the fire to police, arson investigator, and insurance representatives, I felt like a prime suspect on an episode of Columbo. However, this was far from entertaining and, definitely, more terrifying.

We were braving record cold temperatures, even for Michigan, following Kevin's death during that Christmas season. In the crux of it all, I was fielding calls for the fire investigation, talking to homeowner insurance representatives, planning Kevin's celebration of life—he didn't want a funeral—and looking for temporary housing for my children and me. I was too busy to grieve. Where onlookers thought I was being so strong, I had only numbed the pain.

There was no outrunning the emotions that come with grief. Nate had returned to school after the New Year. My daughter was back to work and spending most nights at her boyfriend's house. I had a few more weeks remaining on my personal leave of absence, and the time alone left little distraction from my tears and sadness.

A Wise Woman Seeks Counsel

In February 2018, I attended my first widow group. At 42, I was the youngest woman at a round table that seated six. Everyone's story was similar yet starkly different. All but one or two of the women had been married for over 30 years. Everyone was devastated, whether the death was sudden or expected. Our commonalities were endless tears and loneliness. But no one said anything about anger or guilt. So, I didn't either.

This group wasn't the grief counseling for me. I needed to be able to speak my truth without fear. Personal therapy allowed me to do that. I'd started seeing my therapist, Linda, three years before Kevin passed. Specifically, about six months before his diagnosis. Initially, my visits were for regular marital stuff. After his diagnosis, it became about Kevin's illness and coping with the newfound stress of caregiving.

I was comfortable enough with Linda that I broke down as soon as she closed the door of her office behind me. Through tears, I rehashed the night of the fire. I had told the story so many times it became easy. But talking about the guilt and anger that was consuming my thoughts was not.

Her first question was, "What could you have done?" The truth was I didn't know. The night of the fire, I remembered feeling like Kevin wanted me to go back into the house to retrieve an oxygen tank. But I couldn't. First, it wasn't safe to go back inside a house on fire, and second, a house on fire with flammable oxygen inside was definitely a "No!". Going back in would have been something Kevin would have done if he could have. He was the risk-taker in our relationship.

Needless to say, I didn't risk my life going back in the burning house that night. I'll never know for sure if that's what he expected me to do, but I believe I made the right move.

After that session with my therapist and a lot of prayer, I was closer to accepting that neither Kevin nor I could have saved his life that night. God had already determined the time and the day of Kevin being called home. And nothing I could have done would have changed that.

Don't Fall in the Social Media Expectations.

Over time, my grief began to change course. The anger and guilt subsided, replaced by the overwhelming awareness that my partner, my friend, the man I can be, unequivocally myself with, was gone. This occurred just in time for what would have been our sixth wedding anniversary on March 31, 2018.

I experienced a lot of anxiety up to the day. The last thing I wanted to do was wallow around the house, listening to sad music, and crying. Should I surround myself with family and friends? No, that wasn't authentic to my personality. I decided to spend the day just as we had spent our last two anniversaries. Dinner at the Cheesecake Factory, preceded by a shopping trip at the mall. On our fifth anniversary, Kevin had taken me to the Pandora store and bought me a bangle bracelet and a #5 charm to commemorate the occasion. It was a bittersweet moment. We made it to five years of marriage, ten years together. We both carried the fear that we wouldn't celebrate another anniversary together. In honor of his memory, I purchased a purple charm to add to the bracelet he'd bought me. Purple, a signature color of his beloved fraternity, was his favorite color. I wore the bracelet every day of 2018 and still wear it today.

Throughout the first year of grieving the loss of Kevin, I acknowledged every first without him. Christmas, the very week after he passed, followed by New Year's. Valentine's day was next. Although that wasn't a holiday that we'd celebrated in our relationship, the absence of his random "Happy Valentines' Day, Char" was missed just the same. The fall season brought both of our birthdays, which were in October, followed by the holidays again.

The writer in me had put the proverbial pen to paper. On each notable occasion, I penned an emotion-filled blog post, including my favorite photos of Kevin and me. Those posts received the most likes.

I followed the same course of grieving in 2019- Posting pictures, writing blogs, acknowledging every special occasion that I was sad not to be spending with Kevin. At the top of year three, however, I thought to myself, "How long are you going to do this? "Who is this benefiting?" "Was it genuinely stemming from my grief? Or was I subconsciously trying to reassure family and friends that I was still grieving? These posts were only telling part of the story.

The truth was, eight months into living with the loss of Kevin, the weight of loneliness became real. I wasn't just missing my husband; I was missing the comfort of companionship, the closeness of intimacy. I was missing love.

Kevin and I weren't each other's first love. In fact, when we met, we shared our stories about the first loves who got away. His love that got away was his oldest daughter's mother. Mine was my third high school boyfriend, who I declared would be my husband. We accepted that it was not by chance that these people weren't in our lives anymore. There was no jealousy or resentment between us. And the love that we had for other people didn't diminish the love that we had for each other.

I loved Kevin. I was comforted that he didn't depart this earth questioning my love for him. Throughout our marriage, he often boasted that I loved him like no other. It was true. I loved him fiercely while he lived. And I loved him still. I didn't need to validate that love with social media posts any longer.

The last post I wrote about losing Kevin was after seeing the movie, "A Star is Born." I had seen the original version starring Barbara Streisand when I was a child, and, like most movie enthusiasts, I was eager to see Lady Gaga in the role. All I remembered of the movie is that it was about a rising star falling in love with a man facing the end of his career.

I didn't expect the stream of tears running down my face when Lady Gaga performed the song, "I'll Never Love Again," after her husband committed suicide. The song's lyrics mirrored my emotions when I lost Kevin:

"I wish I could have said goodbye. If I knew it would be the last time, I would have said what I wanted to, maybe even cried for you. If I knew it would be the last time, I would have broke my heart in two, trying to save a part of you.

Don't want to feel another touch, don't want to start another fire. Don't want to know another kiss, no other name falling off my lips.

Don't want to give my heart away to another stranger. Or let another day begin, won't even let the sunlight in. No, I'll never love again..."

"I'll Never Love Again", (Aaron Rairiere, Hillary Lindsey, Lady Gaga, Natalie Henby, 2018)

I immediately downloaded the soundtrack from *Apple Music and listened to that song repeatedly- crying every time. My Facebook post expressed as much. One night, however, I heard the song from a different perspective. It's not by chance that God designed marriage "until death do them part." When one spouse dies, God doesn't expect the remaining spouse to stop living or loving. God is love. He created us to love. We honor Him when we love.

As romanticized and poetic as the lyrics of this song were, I couldn't buy into them. I wanted to live and love again fully. I consider it an honor to God and my husband, who wouldn't have it any other way.

It was time for me to focus on living.

Get Ready, Get Set, Go

In the fall of 2018, I got busy living life. The first thing I did was enroll in a second master's program to pursue a library and information systems degree. It was something I'd been contemplating for five years. Like, I literally had multiple copies of letters of interest for the program in my computer files. On a random Monday, I submitted my application days before the deadline and received my acceptance letter a couple of weeks later.

The experience of witnessing my husband's illness and his death preceded by a house fire convinced me that things couldn't be put off for a tomorrow that may not come.

At the start of my sorority year, I accepted the nomination from one of my line sisters for the chapter journalist position. Honestly, I hadn't expected to win. The woman I was running against had prior experience, and she was a senior member of our chapter. But I'd put the task of running for the position on my long-term to-do list that I kept posted in my cubicle at work. Kevin had served in leadership in his fraternity when he was in college and afterward. He always encouraged me to pursue my full potential. He saw a leader in me. The day I walked up to the podium to give my speech, I knew I was making him proud, which made me happy.

Throughout 2018 and 2019, I was rocking it out professionally, academically, and socially. I didn't miss any events and parties hosted by my sorority. I was involved with my church as well. My son and I went on a 4-day Western Caribbean cruise with high school classmates to celebrate our 25-year reunion. In July 2018, my daughter and her boyfriend got engaged, and we began the exciting mission of wedding planning. The sun had started peeking out from the clouds.

The New Love God Has May Surprise You.

Every part of my life was going well and moving forward except my love life. I was sure that I wasn't ready for a relationship. However, I longed for male companionship. But, as open and available as I was for a man, they weren't approaching me. And I did not understand why.

Here I was, this beautiful, sexy, intelligent, accomplished woman, and not one man at any of the events approached me. It was very discouraging.

Instead of complaining—actually, I did complain a little, I had a little talk with Jesus. He reminded me of something I'd talked to Him about during Kevin's illness.

I was forty when Kevin was diagnosed and, I tried not to think about what my life would be like without him in it, but he talked about his imminent death all the time. In reflecting over my life, I realized that I had spent my entire adult life caring for, nurturing, and loving others—specifically, men and children. I married my first husband at nineteen and gave birth to my daughter at twenty. I divorced him and spent five years in relationships with two-three men, which eventually led me to remarry my ex-husband, thinking life would be easier. That didn't work out, but we did conceive our second child, Nate, before divorcing three years later. I met Kevin shortly after and had been with him ever since.

I recognized an overdependence on relationships with men for fulfillment, and I asked God that if it were His will to call my husband home at this point in our marriage, would He give me the strength and the courage to take some time for myself. I wanted to stop the cycle of relying on relationships with men to make me feel complete. And, nearing the empty nest stage of parenting—a 25-year-old daughter and a 16-year-old son, I wanted to experience loving on myself, learning who I was as a woman outside of children and a husband or boyfriend.

However, when the actual loss occurred and loneliness set in, this desire to engage in self-love flew out the window. Thank God that He knew what I needed. The truth of the matter was that if I met someone during this time of loneliness, I would have fallen back into old patterns of prioritizing others above myself.

God hasn't allowed a special man to come into my life at this time, and I don't believe it's an oversight. He's giving me time to sit in quiet reflection to recognize my worthiness as a child of God and as a woman. To know that I am loved because He is love, and He is always with me means I am never alone.

In the beginning, I avoided those quiet times, usually Saturday and Sunday mornings. I'd find something to watch on T.V., look through text messages for somebody to talk to, scroll my Facebook or Instagram feed. I didn't want what came along with the quiet reflection. Tears over regret over bad decisions and missing the stability of my former life.

Today, I've learned to embrace the times alone. When I awake in my bed, I rejoice, first, that God breathed the breath of life into me. I rejoice that I'm in good health, physically and mentally. I rejoice for the lives of my children, my family, my friends, and, most recently, my granddaughter. There's a lot of love in my life. Then I plan how I'm going to live in my purpose for the day.

About LaCharmine (L.A.) Jefferson

LaCharmine (L.A. Jefferson hails from Michigan and thrives as a Women's Contemporary Novelist and owner of the Indie Publishing Company SQS Publishing. Her debut novel, "*Unfinished Business*," was published in 2009, followed by the sequel, "*Reconciliation to Hell*," published in 2016.

The author and her works have often been showcased in local venues throughout Michigan. Her favorite authors who also inspire her works of fiction are Terry McMillian, Connie Briscoe, and Beverly Jenkins. In 2018, LaCharmine published her first piece of creative non-fiction included in the anthology, "*Daddy: A Reflection of Father-Daughter Relationships*."

L.A. was tragically widowed, December 18, 2017, due to a house fire that robbed her and her children of their home as well. Today, after much prayer, healing, persistence, and retrospect, she lives with her son, rescue dog, and enjoys her latest role as grandmother to a beautiful baby girl- thanks to her daughter. She's also working on her first memoir, detailing a darker side of widowhood.

Connect with LaCharmine (L.A.) Jefferson at authorla46@gmail.com

BY GRACE LIANG

Redefining the look, behavior, and mindset of a widow.

My mom became a widow when she was 44, and she decided her life was over. She has been living an ordinary single widow life for almost 30 years now, still crying and blaming all her troubles on the fact that she is a widow. When I became a widow at 43, I didn't know I had an alternative to my mom's single widowhood.

However, I genuinely believe that no matter what happens in our lives, if we are determined to make the best out of every day by learning, growing, and working through our pain, we will be alright. With this attitude, I found and created a much better life than my mom.

Now, four years after losing my husband Bob, I have healed myself from grief and many past traumas. I have grown stronger, wiser, and happier than before. I found self-love, God's love, and even fell in love again-I recently married my best friend! Life is truly amazing!

You may be wondering how did I get to this point?

Below is my journey.

My late husband Bob and I first met right after I turned 30 years old in Shanghai. Three years later, I moved to America, where we were married. Bob was my first true love, my best friend, and my soulmate. We shared an incredibly happy marriage for ten years, and then I lost him to cancer in January of 2017. After losing him, my whole world was shattered.

Growing up in poverty in China with an abusive mom, I always believed that I was ugly, useless, and never good enough. I felt I only deserved a secondary life since I was such a huge mess. Bob was the first person ever to tell me that I was beautiful, and he was also the first to give me unconditional love (something I had never experienced before). He was the source of my happiness! After he died, the new pain piled on top of the old pain and began crushing me. I thought I would just simply die from my broken heart.

I was so angry but didn't know who I should be angry with! I was also very confused by my life. Why did I have to go through such hard times? Why did my parents give me life and then not love me? Why was it when I finally found my true love that he was taken away? What was my purpose here on earth? Was my purpose just to go through more suffering!?

With many questions, I began the journey of my soul searching. During the first three years after losing my husband, I read almost a hundred self-help books, watched thousands of self-help videos, finished a couple of year-long personal development training programs, and earned a few certificates.

All of these things helped so much that I began to heal. Slowly, I built up a solid foundation of self-love, and I took 100 responsibility in making myself happy- I was amazed by how much I could make myself happy! I ate healthily and slowly dropped off a few medicines. I worked out regularly and got my high school body back. I spent a lot of time alone to reflect on my life and rediscover who I was. I permitted myself to cry, but mostly to be happy! I have become my own source of happiness!

Yet, every time I felt this thing, I call self-love, I became aware of something else- Something much more powerful than my capacity as a human- Something pure and peaceful. It was in this place that I found God!

After that, the Holy Spirit' accelerated the healing process of my stubborn wounds from an abusive childhood, relationships in my 20s, and the loss of my dad during my high school senior year.

I was totally amazed by how wonderful God is! Presently, He is sending so many amazing people and resources into my life to help me heal! I tried everything I knew to heal myself and eliminate limiting beliefs, but I couldn't. Now, when I rest in Jesus Christ and ask him to help me, the right people start to show up, and the right ideas begin to come to me. I have experienced so many "aha" moments and am genuinely enjoying this enlightening journey! I am, what I refer to as, gracefully grieving!

Many people told me that I didn't look like a widow during this process because I was too happy, too powerful, and too put together! So, their assessment got me thinking that it was time to redefine the term WIDOW. Or better yet, determine what an awakened and empowered widow should look like.

Women are traditionally categorized by labels and standards that limit us from growing and thriving. For example, a grieving woman should look sad, lack a spark in their eyes, have dull skin, and shouldn't care about her hair, makeup, or clothes. A grieving woman is expected to be miserable to show how much they love and respect their deceased loved one. These are just some of the biases society has placed upon the grieving woman.

However, a grieving woman CAN still be a powerful woman.

A widow describes a woman whose world was destroyed and shattered without her permission. Simultaneously, she is granted a great opportunity to destroy the shattered life that no longer serves her. Just like a collapsed house after a deadly earthquake, a widow can either repair the house the best she can or totally rebuild a brand-new house from the ground up to meet all of her personal desires and dreams. Which house are you choosing?

Many widows are so overwhelmed and too tired to even think about what they want. Their main goal is to just survive for the moment. You may be asking how, in this messy and stressful world, can a widow transform from barely functioning to taking back control of her life?

The answer is we are NOT that delicate, and we possess the tools to heal ourselves. When God created us, he gave us white blood cells to heal physical illnesses, and he also gave us the power and wisdom to heal our subconscious mind of emotional pain. We ALL have this innate healing power; the problem is, most of us don't really know how to activate or access it.

So how exactly can YOU tap into these powers to heal yourself from loss and past traumas? It only depends on two things. One, you REALLY want to heal, and two, you know HOW to heal.

Being willing to work through your pain is the number one factor in healing yourself. Before knowing God, I could only heal myself up to a certain level. However, after developing my personal relationship with God, I would ask him daily to heal my emotional wounds. I don't know how he does it, but watching myself heal with my own eyes has been amazing!

God easily helps me to forgive and gain compassion for others and myself. Most importantly, he helped me find peace and joy in so many little things! And these little things are the source of my glowing joy!

I believe grieving is like most things in life; it is a SKILL that can be learned and mastered! Suffering less and healing faster requires identifying and removing unnecessary distress caused by our lifelong limiting beliefs.

These limiting beliefs lock us up in guilt, resentment, anger, and depression, impeding the natural healing process.

It's never too late to turn grief into growth! Pray to God to send you the right people and resources to help you learn, rediscover yourself, and heal- Ask for an open mind to try new things (like energy healing)! If you would like to learn more about my "Gracefully Grieving Energy Healing Process," I invite you to do a web-search on, Gracefully Grieving.

I never even knew that I could be this powerful and wise before working through my own grief. I appreciate what life has in store for me. I can proudly say that I am truly living a "have-it-all" life now filled with peace, health, love, wealth, and feeling beautiful!

If a girl like me can heal myself and live my dream life again, you CAN too, with God's help!

Below is an interview I recently had with a magazine on how I transformed my life after loss. You can find more tips here to change your life right away too!

Q 1: How has personal loss helped you find your inner strength in other aspects of your life?

"My attitude toward the unknown has changed, and I am willing to take even more risks because the worst thing has happened to me, but it turned out I was fine. I thought my broken heart would kill me, but I was still breathing, and therefore I still had hope, right?

I also realized that we are not that delicate, and we don't have to accept all the unnecessary suffering if we are willing to heal ourselves. Overall, I know God is with me, and he is helping me go through these hard times. I trust that I am safe, and that life supports me."

Q 2: How have you used the command of your inner power to further your career and reshape your professional life?

"I was a full-time social media lifestyle influencer. When the COVID pandemic started, I realized that the whole world is grieving over either losing a loved one or of our old lifestyle. So many people are hurting, but our culture and schools have never taught us how to grieve properly. Many people are suffering with incomplete grief, and these strong emotions have manifested into many mental and physical illnesses. So, I decided to step up and share my own successful experiences of healing myself from my grief by using my own Gracefully Grieving Energy Healing Process. Now, I am a grief energy healing coach, grief online course creator, and Amazon best-selling author for my book Finding Grace: How to Navigate the Journey from Tragedy to Triumph."

Q 3: What are three tips you'd like to share with someone who has experienced a loss, be it of a loved one, their job, or financial security?

"#1: See grief as a great opportunity to heal yourself not just from this loss but also from all of your previous traumas. The best gift we can give to this world and our loved ones is our true happiness.

A healed person has fewer limiting beliefs to hold them back or resistance to weigh them down. So, success becomes easier since you will reduce your self-sabotaging behaviors.

#2: See grief as a journey of giving birth to your brand-new life and believe that you can and deserve to have it all (peace, health, love, wealth, perfect self-expression, and happiness)! Since your old life was shattered, why should you only try to glue these pieces back together? Instead, build a magnificent life from the ground up! It takes pretty much the same amount of time and energy anyway! It is never too late to answer this question "What do I want to be when I grow up?"

#3: Your grief is not a cold that you can just sit there and wait for it to pass. Grief is a whole package of strong emotions in your body. Emotions are energy in motion, so if you don't intentionally clear the energy path to let them pass through you, they will be stuck in your body and manifest into physical illnesses like weight problems and heart problems or as emotional blocks like money blocks and relationship blocks. Overall, everyone has their own built-in healing power within their subconscious minds, but not everyone knows how to tap into this power to heal themselves. Like everything else in life, grieving is a skill that can be learned and mastered. When you master your grieving, you are not just able to suffer less and heal faster, but you will learn how to tap into the power of grieving and come out of it stronger, wiser, and happier!"

With faith, love, and dedication to honor God, your life, and your deceased loved one, you will soon be able to heal yourself. Just imagine on your wedding anniversary that you are thinking about your late husband. You have been staring at your wedding picture and internally scanning your body for the pain over losing him. However, all you can find is the love and joy he has brought to your heart! You are now able to look at your wedding picture for a great length of time without hurting. All you feel is the smile on your face without having to fake it forcing yourself to smile!

And from that moment, you are HEALED!

About Grace Liang

Grace Liang is a Certified Jack Canfield Success Principles Speaker/ Trainer, Grief Energy Healing Coach, Emotion Code Practitioner, and Certified RIM Facilitator. She is also the #1 New Release, Amazon Best Selling Author of *Finding Grace: How to Navigate the Journey from Tragedy to Triumph.*

Grace's personal story of living her dream life after overcoming poverty, family abuse, domestic violence, moving to a foreign country, and losing her husband to cancer will bring you hope and inspire you to thrive! She focuses on teaching women to suffer less and heal faster by using her *Gracefully Grieving Energy Healing Process,* to turn grief to growth and live a joyful life again! Grace is newly married and resides in Birmingham, Michigan.

Connect with Grace Liang at gracel@colorandgrace.com

TRUE LOVE NEVER DIES

BY MONICA MORGAN

True Love Never Dies

I knew this was going to be one of the worst days of my life. Upon entering the private hospice's family room, I was so depleted that I couldn't even pretend to be strong. All I could think about was G. in the other room slipping away from me. Thank goodness Emma, Alysyn, and Brittney were present; I was grateful and flashed them a smile. They were my true support system at a time when I was tired of being strong- Honestly, I didn't know how to be anything else.

As the day wore on, a myriad of emotions seized my self-control and seeped out as anger and sadness- All I wanted to do was run into my husband's room, get into his arms, and cry! I couldn't do that- No. I had to share G. with the world. After all, there were others who wanted to say "Goodbye," and as usual, I had to be gracious.

"You got flowers," Emma said gently. "Open the card."

It was then that I looked over and saw the red roses and the balloon that said, "I love you."

Flowers? Who'd send flowers like that? My husband wasn't even cold yet.

"Come on," Emma chided. "Open the card."

"No!" I screamed silently. I'm tired of not doing what I want. Besides, who was insensitive enough to send something so inappropriate at a time like this?

After my mental tirade, I shot Emma a look that said, "I don't care about those flowers." Yet, she insisted softly, "Open the card..." gently handing it to me.

I took the small envelope from her and pulled out the card tucked inside. After reading the message, my hand started trembling, and I felt like the wind had been knocked out of me. Stark disbelief followed by an abrupt stream of tears rendered me apathetic- Someone probably hugged me, but I can't be sure.

At that point, I began reminiscing, remembering how it wasn't love at first sight. As a matter of fact, G's business persona and immense stature actually scared me. We met at a luggage carousel in the airport after my friend Pam pointed him out. Gathering up all my strength, I boldly approached him-

"Hello, Mr. Holiefield. I'm Monica Morgan. It's ok to say 'no,' but please be courteous and say something."

He looked at me, perplexed, and then flashed a smile. "Miss Morgan, I'm not sure what you're talking about," he said, reaching into his pocket and pulling out a card.

"However, I'll be back in my office next week, and you can set up an appointment with my secretary."

Either he deserved an Academy Award, or he really had no idea what I was talking about. Now I was perplexed because I recently met with two of his colleagues. The purpose of that meeting was to discuss their sponsorship for a book I was publishing. Afterward, it was relayed that Mr. Holiefield was the hold-up in closing the deal.

Judging from his expression, I realized he didn't know what I was talking about, but his gentle manner and bright smile told me that he would find out.

As suggested, I made and kept an appointment to meet with the gentleman. When I reached his office, there was soft jazz playing, and he had on the most hypnotic cologne. He told me that he wasn't aware of the potential sponsorship but would talk to a few people and let me know.

Being an introvert, I was nervous but felt confident that I'd locked in the sponsorship. Unfortunately, Mr. Holiefield would call with news contrary to my expectations. He further explained the state of his industry and what it might potentially suffer. Therefore, it wasn't a good time to buy a book sponsorship. He offered me a teaching position instead, training kids in photography. I graciously declined his offer because my focus was on publishing the coffee table book. Besides, I realized that I needed to stay away from him. His personality was magnetic, and we both knew there was a certain chemistry—It wouldn't be hard for me to become attached to him. But, as luck would have it, I learned that he wasn't available. Yet, I couldn't get the gentle giant out of my mind. He sent me a few texts throughout the following year, but I kept my responses short and sweet knowing that our timing was somehow off.

Flashback to 1994—I was in Johannesburg, South Africa, photographing people who registered to vote in the first "All-Race" elections. Although it was a foregone conclusion that Mandela would be president, the morning moved at a snail's pace in an atmosphere of silence—Hard to believe, but I actually felt bored. Then suddenly, I heard a loud noise followed by a succession of noises. Simultaneously, what once was an orderly scene of voter registration quickly shifted into a chaotic scrambling, and people screaming in their native tongues!

I thought someone was shooting and immediately took cover behind a van door! From this vantage point, I surmised that many people had looked up into the sky just minutes before the bomb struck. Almost mechanically, I touched the cross that my grandmother had placed around my neck before I left for South Africa, and I ran toward the bomb's aftermath, clutching my camera.

My images depicted people who were suffering, people who were bleeding, and people who had died. There was one woman, wrapped in a towel, whose face was covered in blood. I was later told that she was searching for her lost child. My image of her ran on the front page of newspapers around the world.

That tragic circumstance caused my career to take off! I was no longer the photographer next door; I was internationally renowned. From that point, I photographed presidents, heads of state, icons, celebrities, corporate executives, 911, and Katrina.

However, during my success, I realized that I wasn't fearless like many people thought; I was lonely. I took chances with my life because up until now, my career was the most important thing in the world to me- but my prince was nowhere in sight. You see, as a teen, I'd read all these *Harlequin Romance novels, believing that my prince would find me. Well- my prince never arrived, but a 'general' did. He was so much better than the prince I always envisioned.

His name was General Holiefield, and not only was he debonair; he was also a skilled arbitrator who negotiated the deal to save Chrysler Motor Company. This act was no small feat; therefore consider, if you have a family member employed by Chrysler or who receives a company pension, it is because of my husband's negotiation skills.

His capacity to effect change was humbling- It made me realize that just as his dedication and expertise qualified him to save thousands of jobs, his love and kindness qualified him to save me as well.

Billy Dee Williams had a line in the movie *Mahogany* that went, "Success is nothing, nothing without someone you love to share it with."

Exactly a year later, that line would describe our next chapter.

"Let's get married."

"Married?" I thought. The question arrested my comprehension, causing me to pause like a deer caught in headlights. Who wants to get married after a recent divorce?

"Or we can live together." I countered.

He swiftly said, "No, I don't play house. I want you to have it all."

Again, I was speechless and couldn't say anything but, "Yes!"

And then he took me in his arms and said, "And you're no longer going to chase any bombs because you have someone who loves you."

From that point on, we were practically inseparable. We traveled the world, riding elephants in Thailand and looking for Hippopotamuses in Africa. It didn't matter if we were in the grocery store; we had fun.

General even went with me to the cosmetic store and sat in the corner as I played with various shades. It really didn't matter where we were, as long as we were together. We learned ballroom dancing, and every time he took me in his arms and swung me around, I felt protected, safe, and loved.

Then one day, he felt stomach pain. We thought that it was something he had eaten. After multiple hospital visits and stays, a surgeon removed his gallbladder still the pain continued. The doctors assured us it was healing pain.

Despite his discomfort, G. kept going; he was strong and determined to press through the pain.

It was about 3:30 a.m. Thanksgiving morning, our first as a married couple. He was making the turkey and dressing, and I was making the side dishes. For some reason, he thought that I could cook. Little did he know that I was at the grocery store the night before asking a woman for instructions on how to make mac and cheese. You can ask my family, they'll tell you I can't cook. But he said, "I could, put my foot in some greens." That's what you call true love.

"Moni, if you're getting up, would you cut the oven off and leave the turkey in it?"

"Are you sure it's ok to leave it in the oven?...Ok," and I must have turned over and gone back to sleep — abandoning my intention to get up and get something to drink.

Imagine my surprise the following morning when I saw that the turkey was still baking. So, I quickly retrieved the crispy bird out of the oven — needing G. to think I had removed it hours earlier. My heart was pounding as I worked on the side dishes while imagining a ruined holiday because G. was going to be mad at me.

When he saw the turkey, he studied its crunchy exterior. "Hmm, it's a little done; I should've listened to you and taken it out of the oven."

The way he said it was so sweet, I felt guilty and confessed on the spot. "It's my fault; I didn't cut the oven off."

Immediately I thought of those "I Love Lucy" episodes when Ricky was infuriated by Lucy's antics.

"It's ok."

Ok? Who says that? I pondered quizzically, "What do you mean it's ok?"

"It was my responsibility. I'm the one that should've made sure it was taken out of the oven, not you."

He wasn't angry.

General taught me how to have patience because I didn't have any. Through him, I learned how to be softer, kinder, and gentler- to be the bigger person. He never pushed his ideologies on me. I learned by watching him. He always told me to do me. You see, if he believed in something, he didn't expect me to agree with him or believe in it, too, simply because I was his wife.

He wanted me to come around to his way of thinking on my own. Yet if I didn't, it was ok because that's not why he loved me- He loved me for me.

During the course of G's discomfort, we visited a doctor who later became our friend. He gently suggested that G go into the hospital through the emergency department, have some blood drawn, and an exploratory scope procedure. Dr. Gazeryerli's gentle manner made us think it was routine.

General never went to a doctor's appointment or stayed in a hospital without me; this time would be no different. I woke that morning comforted by his big bear hug. It was December 4, 2014. The day my heart was crushed.

This doctor came in who we didn't initially recognize. He turned out to be the surgeon who removed G's gallbladder a few weeks earlier.

I got up quickly and stood next to my husband's bed.

"Hey, big fella. Wake up." He then looked at me and said, "Have a seat."

There was a thick heaviness in the quiet room before he spoke.

"We found nine tumors in your liver and one in your pancreas. I'm so sorry."

He didn't even say General's name. My heart stopped, and as I gathered breath, I was able to ask, "You caught it early, right? You just took his gallbladder out; you had to know."

"I'm so sorry," he responded blankly.

General and I believed in God and the power of prayer. We prayed as we had never prayed in our lives, knowing that to have the prayers answered, we had to believe that they would be. Therefore, G opted not to share his diagnosis. "Moni, don't let those doctors tell me anything negative." I don't want to hear any bad news blocking my belief that God's going to bring me through this."

He was in the hospital, and we had just said a prayer when his doctors came in and took me out in the hall—they knew his wishes.

"His kidneys are failing, and there's nothing else we can do. We need to put him in palliative care in the hospice."

I felt as if I'd been sucker-punched, knocked down, but if you can look up, you can get up. You never know how strong you are until being strong is your only solution. I loved my husband so deeply that I couldn't fall apart because of the doctor's report. Instead, I went back to him and played "Best of Me" by Anthony Hamilton, took his hand, and we ballroom danced as he lay in the hospital bed. God had us.

Hospice was located on the other side of Karmanos Cancer Institute, which was a long walk down the hall. As my grandfather once said, "It is better to act than to react." It was time to tell his family and his world.

Portia, the Hospital Chaplain, came daily with prayers and a ray of sunshine; sometimes, she even sang. Our dear friends, Alysyn and Brittney, slept in the private waiting room. People came from all walks of life to see him.

I called Eddie LeVert and asked if he could please contact Otis Williams from The Temptations no matter what it took. I had arranged a meeting with Otis and my husband during the Christmas holiday, and he never stopped talking about meeting his childhood idol. Eddie indeed found Otis, and Otis called General almost every day after. I pretended not to hear when he said that he should have asked Otis could he sing a song with him. G could sing, but I'm glad he hadn't asked me to help make that desire come true.

I remembered a dream of mine that G. made come true. It took place as we stood in a small church in Toledo, Ohio, with eight of our closest relatives and friends. That was the day I became his wife, and he sang "When I Found You" by BeBe and CeCe Winans. My response was the lyrics to Celine Dion's song "Because You Loved Me."

We laughed and joked with each other through the ceremony, and it was the happiest day of my life. Seven months later, we had a ceremony at St. Mark's Basilica in Venice, Italy. Still, it was nothing like the moment when I actually became his wife in that modest church in Toledo. We had the first wedding because G wanted to make sure that we were married and there wouldn't be any red tape in another country.

We took a Norwegian Cruise to other ports in Italy, Greece, Turkey, France, and Spain.

Unfortunately, my mind was being tugged away from fonder memories by doctors who told me that it would be any minute. He was sleeping all the time, and he wasn't fully cognizant.

This moment was when I pulled the card from its envelope and read the content over and over again. How was it possible? The card said, "Boo, my heart is filled with love for you."

The tears started to flow, and I no longer cared about, nor could I maintain the appearance of, being strong. Unbeknownst to me, General made arrangements with Brittney to have flowers sent to me when he no longer could. He quietly slipped away, the evening of March 10, 2015, as I held him in my arms, with "Somewhere" from The Temptations playing in the background.

There's a place for us
Somewhere a place for us
Peace and quiet and open air
Wait for us, somewhere
There's a time for us
Someday there's a time for us
Time together with time to spare
Time to learn, time to care
Someday, somewhere
We'll find a new way of living
Somewhere

There's a place for us
There's a time and place for us
Hold my hand and we're halfway there
Hold my hand and I'll take you there
Somehow, someday, somewhere
Someday, I will show it
Somewhere

Somewhere [The Temptations version]
Source: LyricFind
Songwriters: Robert Westerholt / Sharon J. Den Adel

Here are ways that I've been able to remain resilient:

- I believe, "If you can look up, you can get up," and that's what you need to do. It's so easy to stay in bed with the blinds drawn and the covers over your head, but I urge you to get up and look for some sunshine.
- Breathe- When a painful memory or reality hits you hard, stop and breathe through it.
- Reflect on if the roles were reversed, you'd want your spouse to live, to be happy. Believe that's what your spouse wants for you.
- Instead of being sad on the anniversary of your spouse's passing, as Dr. Pauline J. Furman says, "Celebrate that your spouse lived, instead of dwelling on their death."
- During your relationship, take lots of photos (even on bad hair days.) I'm grateful to my assistant and friend, photographer, Cyndi Elledge, for the many images she captured of us. I can relive my moments with my soulmate.

- Don't wait for tomorrow; sometimes tomorrow doesn't come. I recommend saving special voicemails, too.

Here is a portion of one of my cherished voicemails from General: "Hey Moni, I just want to tell you that I really, really appreciated you this morning. You know I don't always say what I should or show the feelings that I should when I should, and I apologize for that as well...

"But above all, I just wanted to say thank you for making my morning special and showing me so much love. I want you to know my heart is just running over with love for you.

There's nothing I won't do for you, you're the love of my life, and I love you so much baby, I love you so, so very much. If I could snatch the stars from the heavens, I'd give them all to you, every one of them, and I'd make a crown for you; I really would because you mean just that much to me. Stay as you are, continue to love me, and I swear I'll always love you, and I'll never do anything to hurt my baby, never. My credo is to make you happy and to do all the wonderful things that I can in this life for you."

Part of my resilience is knowing and remembering that I'll always have this.

My story with General Holiefield is not over.

He sends me signs.

True love never dies.

About Monica Morgan

Monica Morgan is a Michigan native with a drive to tell visual stories, and is undisputedly among the world's most highly accomplished, and sought-after African American photographers. With a lifetime of world-class photography as backdrop, Morgan is available on the world stage, teaching and speaking to audiences globally. Morgan's story features personal tragedy and turmoil, such as being accidentally shot at close range, losing the love of her life to cancer, and then, being incarcerated. These turbulent events serve to make her ever determined to aim high, and stay a stronger voice, speaking to those in need of inspiration and advocacy.

Monica Morgan has photographed countless celebrities, heads of state, and many world events that have shaped life as we know it. Morgan's WireImage.com contract establishes international access to her images for editors, entertainment, and news media.

Connect with Monica Morgan at
monica@monicamorganphotography.com

CHANGELESS LOVE

BY WILMA PARHAM

Changeless Love

To suddenly find myself a widow after 54 years of marriage is hard enough; being hit with a worldwide pandemic shortly afterward is more than hard; it's devastating! How can I remain true to my faith when my life, as well as the world around me, is so uncertain? There is just one answer; God keeps His promises.

God said:

- I will Provide for you – Matthew 6:11; Philippians 4:19; Psalms 23
- I will Comfort you – John 14:16
- I will Protect you – Psalms 5:11
- I will give you Peace – Luke 24:36; Isaiah 53:5
- I will never leave you nor forsake you – Psalm 9:10

God has kept these promises to me, especially over the past 17 months.

My story begins in 1983 when my husband and I were in the process of purchasing a home. At the same time, I realized that my mother's health was failing. On the weekends, I would stop by to visit with her, and several times noticed there was no food cooked on the stove. This was unusual. When I asked what she had eaten, she would say a peanut butter sandwich while fervently trying to convince me that she just loved peanut butter.

I knew something was wrong, and then one day, she called me at work to say she was going to have my sister look for her a senior citizen apartment. She felt it was time to move out of her home. When I asked if that was what she REALLY wanted to do, she cried, stating that she did not want to burden anyone. I explained that she was not a burden and informed her that my husband Dewey and I were buying a house. Impetuously, I invited her to come and live with us, but after hanging up realized that I should have talked to my husband first.

I could not wait for him to get home that evening so I could discuss it with him. As it turned out, Dewey was very gracious and had no objections at all. I was so relieved and almost felt guilty, knowing that if the shoe was on the other foot, I could not have agreed to live with his mother.

Two years after moving into our home Dewey called on a Friday evening to let me know he got injured at work. I listened in shock as he explained how a heavy, steel rod broke off his truck and nearly knocked him un-conscience. The incident occurred as he was attempting to unload cars at a Pennsylvania dealership. When the dealership owner rushed him to a local clinic, Dewey was dazed, spitting up blood, and in a lot of pain. On top of that, he needed to get home because he needed additional medical treatment.

Despite the urgency of the situation, Dewey's supervisor wanted him to remain in Pennsylvania to continue delivering cars the next day because the Teamsters were about to strike. Needless to say, he had no compassion for my husband.

I've considered that we live in a cruel world where many companies reward loyal workers who make them millions of dollars but quickly forget that loyalty should an illness or injury occur. One can easily be defeated if you cannot fight for yourself. Being anchored in Jesus Christ is the only way to survive.

Somehow Dewey made it home but only received checks for the next two weeks before the company cut his money off.

This was the beginning of a long journey of trials and suffering.

As it turned out, Dewey's injuries were not minor. His X-rays revealed a severe Closed Head Injury, and the doctor's prognosis gave little hope. The doctors rendered him totally disabled. Therefore, he was required to make weekly visits to the company's medical clinic and be treated by his physician as well. On two occasions, he was hospitalized as an inpatient. It would be over a year before Dewey's checks started coming in again, but by the grace of God, I continued to work and was able to keep the bills paid. I never missed a mortgage or utility payment; all bills were paid on time, and I did not borrow money from anyone. God is my provider!

Yet, sadly, at forty-two years of age, Dewey ended up retiring on disability. During this course of events, my mother was diagnosed with Parkinson's disease. These circumstances brought about unimaginable trials while I worked, went to school, and raised a teenage son.

I started attending Support Group Meetings with Dewey at a local hospital. The spouses met in a separate room, and I remember sitting there, listening to them seemingly whine and complain about their situation. One lady in the support group described how her husband, who had always been very thoughtful, now gets out of the car and no longer opens the door for her. She went on to describe in detail, various other personality changes. It all sounded like whining to me.

Some of them were chain smokers, and the room would be filled with smoke. It was all I could do to sit through two or three meetings before I quit going. However, Dewey continued. Unfortunately, he was lethargic most days and spent a lot of time sleeping. His peers, I noticed, moved like zombies under the influence of strong medication. Then, people in this support group began passing away, one-by-one. I knew without a doubt that Dewey had to come off of the heavy medication he was taking.

This was the second major hurdle in our marriage.

Behold, "Now" is the Day of Salvation.
I am so thankful for the day my friend Barbra invited my husband and I to her church. Although we were both Christians, we lived a worldly life. That day when the

Pastor opened the doors of the church, my friend Barbra stood up and reached out her hand for us to follow her up to the alter. We were at a low point in our lives, feeling defeated by his illness. I had never been in a Baptist Church before and did not realize what was happening. I thought she was going to tell the Pastor that we were coming up for prayer, but to my surprise, the Pastor looked at us and said, "Do you believe that Jesus Christ is the only begotten son of God, and that He died on the cross for your sins, and that he was buried, and arose on the third day"?

The church was silent, and all eyes were on us. I began to get nervous because though I was a believer, I didn't know if saying "Yes," also meant joining that church. It was our first time there, and I didn't know if I wanted to become a member. Dewey immediately spoke up loudly, saying, "Yes."

The Pastor then repeated the gospel to me, but it was like I was in a daze; I stood there feeling that I needed to repent of all my sins first.

Finally, I said, "Yes," recalling that Jesus just wants us to "believe in our hearts and confess with our mouth." (Romans 10:9) That was a real turning point in our lives because this time, we really started living for Christ. The following Sunday was Baptismal Sunday. Neither of us had been baptized before, and I felt compelled to fully repent before going into the water. Therefore, I spent the entire week humbly before God, praying, and repenting of every sin I could think of.

Dewey prayed as well, and God did miraculous things in our life after that. *This invitation started us on our way to a new life in Christ. We did not look back.*

If I have to mark the time, I suppose it was a year or so after Dewey's accident, when we held hands and approached the Alter in church. Together, we engaged in travailing prayer before God, asking Him to bring Dewey off the medication and to make him whole again. We also asked for God's wisdom in taking care of his health. God's word says we can "come boldly unto the throne of grace, that we may receive mercy and find grace to help in our time of need." Hebrews 4:16

That prayer began a quality of life that he would not have known otherwise.

It was then that we trusted God and slowly weaned him off the medication. Little did we know that he would subsequently enjoy thirty-three plus years of life, where he could attend and serve in the church, socialize, travel, shop and dress, without medication. But God!

When We Met

Dewey and I met just prior to attending a picnic on Memorial Day, shortly after my 16th birthday. He stepped out of his car so that we could be introduced, and his smile captured my heart. We began dating shortly after my seventeenth birthday, and as it got closer to my 18th birthday, we started discussing marriage. It seemed inevitable at that point because we were inseparable. Dewey was determined to ask my father for my hand in marriage right away. I tried to get him to hold off until after graduation, but he was set on having a big wedding and therefore knew the planning had to get underway. He approached my father one day when he was sitting on the porch. They had a pleasant conversation, and my father gave his approval without hesitation, but with a few rules. From then on, in addition to graduation planning, we were making wedding plans.

August 22, 1964 was the date. It seemed the closer it got to 4:00 p.m., the harder it rained. The rain was a disappointment to me, but despite it, the church was filled. When I said, "I Do," I truly meant it, and I believe he did too. Our marriage was based upon love and trust. Nothing in life or death could ever take that away. We were blessed to have a marriage that lasted 54 years.

The First Hurdle

I knew there would be problems when we received a knock on our door on our wedding night. Having decided to delay our honeymoon, we slipped out of the after-party at midnight and retired to our new home - an upper flat on the west side of Detroit. After we were in bed, someone began knocking on the door. When the knocking became incessant, it was harder to ignore, forcing Dewey to get out of bed, get dressed, and answer. As it turns out, it was my mother-in-law with two carloads of her closest friends.

"Just let us in for a few minutes," she insisted. "We won't stay long."

I couldn't believe my ears. Dewey's mother was just there to show off our house full of new furniture and wedding gifts. She and her friends were late getting to the after-party because she had taken them to her house for dinner before bringing them to our gathering. Granted, she was an excellent cook, but so were my uncle and grandmother, who hosted the after-party. Shame on her! This interruption was the first of many incidents and unannounced visits from my mother-in-law. The Lord called her home suddenly, in 1972, shortly before Christmas.

During those first six years, our most joyous moment was when our son Marlon was born in 1970. Marlon was almost two years old when Dewey's mother passed. My father-in-law had never been a problem. He was a kind, quiet-natured man like my father.

There is a lesson to be learned in every trial that we go through. My struggles to live in harmony with my husband's mother helped me to be the best mother-in-law that I could be. Therefore, the Lord gave me the best daughter-in-love that I could ever wish for, and she birthed my two beautiful granddaughters! To God, be the glory!

As the years progressed, I began noticing changes in Dewey's behavior. Ironically, I observed changes similar to those described by the women I sat with at the support group. His sense of reasoning and decision-making was of concern to me. So I gradually took over initiating household maintenance projects and handling business matters. I also did nearly all of the driving. He did not seem to have a problem with it since he still managed his own pocket money.

Imagine the pain that I experienced by burying these feelings deep inside, never discussing them, just going along with what he wanted. The man that I married was now someone else. Oh, he functioned normally and seemed the same to those on the outside, but he wasn't the guy I fell in love with—the guy who showered me with love and attention. He now made excuses to stay at home and discouraged social gatherings.

In recent years, more personality changes became evident. I couldn't help but notice when Dewey stopped taking time to match his suit, socks, tie, handkerchief, and shoes before going to church. Dewey was six feet, one inch tall and believed in being neat and coordinated when he went out. Now, he would put on whatever was handy and did not need pressing. He had a huge collection of suits to choose from, but he started to wear the same or similar black suits often, and if he did not feel like putting on a tie, he would pull out one of his African outfits for church. He was still neat, but I could see he just did not have the energy to be selective any more.

I thank God that He allowed Dewey to function so well for so long. Later on, a couple of mild strokes contributed to bouts of irritability. He was no longer outgoing and full of conversation. He talked more to close friends with whom he was familiar, but at times it was as if he did not know what to say to others, so he was silent. Still, despite it all, I continued to shower him with the love and attention he needed, fix his favorite meals, and keep our home a loving place.

His heart became weak; a few years before his passing, he had a valve replacement. As his physical health changed, I would educate myself concerning his condition learning how to best take care of him. Love is what love does!!

The last six months before he passed, he was determined to accept all invitations to family dinners, graduations, friends' social gatherings, etc., even though he barely had the energy to get dressed. I found out the day before he passed that his heart was only pumping at 10 percent, which I realize was the reason for his lack of energy. He never complained.

In January of 2019, I was on my way to Dewey's hospital room at Providence hospital around 8:25 a.m. when I heard a "code blue" over the loudspeaker. The room number sounded like it could be his room, but I was not sure. I started walking faster and faster, and sure enough, when I turned the corner, all I could see were doctors and nurses flooding the room. The nurse at the desk saw the look on my face and stopped me, asking who I was. I told her, and she said I could not go in.

"What's wrong?" I asked.

"The nurse could not get a pulse." was her answer.

The rest is all a blur. The medical team worked on Dewey for a half-hour before declaring him deceased. The doctor said his heart muscle was just too weak. I thought the pain I felt was more than I could bear. But God knows, and he doesn't allow something like this to happen until we can handle it. Had I not stopped to call my daughter-in-love from the car before coming in, I would have been there sooner. But I was thankful that she was near the hospital and could come to be with me.

Why couldn't I have been there? Why didn't I get there a little earlier? Why didn't I stay last night? All these things went through my mind, but God is in control.

A widow must be able to adjust to a new life by seeking God for direction and purpose. This meant trying to figure out who I was. Many people will quickly offer advice or suggestions when death occurs, but you are at a most gullible stage, so be aware. The best advice I received was from other widows who agreed on one point: don't make any major decisions for at least a year. Some had made quick decisions to move or sell their homes, only to regret it later.

My cousin Joan suggested that I join a support group for widows led by her friend Millie. Being a strong Christian, I thought I was ok, but I felt led to attend while seeking God for direction. It proved to be a decision that helped me get through the grieving process.

The group consisted of 12 women that formed a haven for widows to share what is on their hearts without being judged or feeling alone. They are loving, caring women who welcomed me in with open arms. Their empathy and compassion is unmistakable. We study from a workbook backed up by Scripture that challenged us to dig deep within our feelings. It helped us to face our fears and apprehensions head-on.

The following is a result of my soul-searching journey.

How Can I Be Resilient?

- Knowing that Dewey was saved gives me a sense of peace because I know that his eternal relationship with God is secure, and I know I will see him again.
- Knowing that I did all I could for him is what gives me the peace of God.

God knows I was a good and faithful wife.

- I certainly could not blame or question God for his timing in calling Dewey home because I am incredibly grateful for the 54 years that He did exceeding abundantly above all that we ask or think, according to the power that works in us".
  Ephesians 3:20

The peace of God removes fear.

- I believe God rejoices when we trust Him enough to enjoy life lightheartedly. We cannot be joyful when we carry the weight of the world on our shoulders. Dewey was lighthearted. He enjoyed laughing.

As I mentioned before, being a widow means trying to find out who you are. I sort of lived in Dewey's shadow, joking that my purpose here was to be his wife because he had so many ways that I felt other women would not be able to deal with, like not helping around the house. I didn't nag him about these things because I could see there was no changing him.

I spend many quiet moments reflecting on the good times, like how we enjoyed traveling, attending family reunions, and enjoying our granddaughters. People always seemed to remember him; while on the other hand, they didn't usually remember me until I was identified as Dewey's wife. That did not bother me a bit because I was happy to be his wife. My heart is filled with gratitude to God for hearing our prayer that day and giving us many good years to travel the world and enjoy life before his personality changed. I reflect on those good years. After all, the Dewey I married passed a few years before he took that last breath on January 3, 2019, but true love never dies. He remained vibrant and happy until the end, so that's what matters to me.

Wisdom Keys:

1. Consider attending Grief Seminars offered by your local funeral home.
2. Join a trusted Support Group
3. Immerse yourself in God's Word by joining Bible Study groups and by the consistent study of His word.
4. Set aside a regular time for prayer each morning.
5. Allow yourself some quiet time daily to meditate and hear God speaking to your heart.
6. Know that Christians grieve too – everyone's experience is different.
7. There is no time limit in the grief process, so don't let anyone else decide for you when it should be over.
8. Keep busy doing whatever interests you.
9. Exercise and take care of your health. Exercise is known to release stress.

About Wilma Parham

Wilma Parham was born and raised in Detroit, Michigan graduating from Detroit's Business school – The High School of Commerce. She earned a BBA degree in Computer Information Systems from Davenport University and currently resides in Oak Park, Michigan.

In 2005, she retired from her IT Business Consultant position after 37 years of employment with AAA Michigan, where she developed and maintained corporate software for the company's Finance Department. Then sadly, in January of 2019, Wilma became a widow after spending 54 years in love and devotion to her husband, Dewey.

Currently, she owns WP Jewelry & Craft Solutions, LLC, and is co-founder of Heart Expressions Ministry. Wilma is a born-again, Spirit-filled woman who serves as a Prayer Warrior for a local television network and helps victims of domestic violence and exploitation through mentoring, coaching, teaching, and sharing.

Connect with Wilma Parham at wdew1542@sbcglobal.net

A RENEWED MIND OF A WIDOW WARRIOR

BY BEATRICE YESUFU

Reclaiming Identity

It was Saturday, May 21, 2011, exactly 48 hours before Beatrice's thirty-fifth birthday. The fact that she would not celebrate this year was trivial compared to her life's current demands. She dressed herself quickly with her three children and headed to the Lagos State University Teaching Hospital where her husband, Moses, was a patient in the facility and anti-cipated his wife's daily visits. However, on Friday, he assured Beatrice that he would wait for her; little did she know Moses meant he would still be alive when she returned the next day. How curious, she thought, especially when they sought God continuously for his complete healing.

Upon her arrival, they prayed together and confessed their faith in Christ Jesus, their Lord, and redeemer.

1 John 1:7 says,

"But if we walk in the light, as he is in the light, we have fellowship with one another, and the blood of Jesus Christ, his Son cleanest us from all sin."

After prayer, Moses asked to see his elder children, Joy, and Joshua as his illness had kept them apart for a month. When they stepped forward to lay eyes on their ailing father, he looked at them and then looked at Beatrice, who said, "Moses, pray for your children."

He, in turn, responded, "I have already prayed for them before now; take them out of this room."

She could feel that her husband's departure was near and granted his request by moving the children to the reception area. They barely understood what was taking place at the tender ages of 6, 5, and 1. In all honesty, neither did she, for just three days prior, they sang hymns and read the Bible for 5 hours as her husband desired. Moses loved reading the Bible; it was a part of his daily routine. What she cherished was every moment they spent together as husband and wife.

After the children left, Moses requested a bottle of Coca-Cola, which the nurse ok-ed because his sugar level was low. He seemed happy drinking his beverage, and when he finished, he stopped breathing. Moses Akahome, her dear, sweet husband, finally slept a sleep of peace.

Beatrice vividly remembered Moses telling her during their time of courtship how he marked every one of his achievements by drinking a bottle of Coca-Cola. To know that he drank his favorite beverage before he died told her that he considered his life to be an achievement. She was sure that he was now rejoicing in heaven.

The Trauma, Tragedy, and Triumph.
As my beloved Moses slept in the Lord, it still didn't seem quite real, but more like a dream. Often, I awoke confused but not dismal-I craved tears but could not cry because God shined his light upon me, and I was at peace.

What did disturb me, however, was that within 20 minutes of Moses' death, my sister showed up very annoyed, saying, "Sister, your brother-in-law called from your phone number requesting that I come and take you from here to your father's house. He was swift to caution that tradition demands you can't go back to your husband's house until after his burial."

Suddenly, the haze of grief vanished as I realized the conspiracy to rob me had begun! Three months earlier, Moses told me that I must return to our residence on the same day that he dies. I must never allow fear of any kind to push me out of my home.

Of course, I could never imagine him anywhere else but beside me. So, I replied, "Love, please stop; we are together. You will not die, you will recover, and we shall always be a happy family."

In response, he said, "Go and get your pen and diary; I need to tell you what will happen after my death."

So, I did all that he asked, writing down the essential facts about his culture and how things worked."

The details of his explanation were sick and revolting at times; still, I held on to the timbre of his voice-listening.

"Oft times," Moses explained, "the widow's human rights are violated. After I am dead, the women of my family will beat you, and they may remove your clothes and lock you up in a dark room. When they wash my body, the bathwater shall be given to you to drink. Beatrice, my love, I don't want you to go through any of that."

His eyes held mine until I absolved his doubt with an affirmative nod. Only then did he continue.

"Do not allow my body to be taken away from you. If you remember everything I am telling you, you will not suffer at the hands of my people."

He told me many things, what to do, say, and how to react at each stage in this dreadful process. When Moses was sure that I understood, he made me promise that I would stay with our children, at any cost, to which I agreed.

This knowledge settled like a bitter glaze on top of the daily indignities suffered by widows. Sadly, I learned it was commonplace in Nigerian culture for widows to be humiliated, victimized, and robbed. The culprits were usually greedy in-laws, and one of their more gainful ploys was to remove the widow from her home with threats and intimidation. Next, the vacant property was combed for valuables, robbed, and the widow becomes destitute. In some cases, their children become orphans.

These atrocities happened to thousands of widows; some are even sent to an early grave.

I refused to be dragged out of my home like trash! No-Not this widow! In Psalm 3:6, the promise of God says,

"I will not be afraid of ten thousand people that have set themselves against me."

Therefore, against tradition, I declined my sister's request and returned to my house the same day Moses died. I could still hear his advice clinging to my ears, "Beatrice, give no room for them to deal with you, and make no mistake; the only culture I know to be the truth is the word of God."

During that time, Nahum 1:9 became my mantra of strength.

"What do ye imagine against the Lord? He will make an utter end; affliction shall not rise up the second time."

Isaiah 41: 29 is the verse that usually followed.

"He giveth power to the faint; and to them that have no might he increases strength" Praise be to God!

With God's help, my strength increased, and Moses' instructions became a guide to lead me out of my limitation. My ideas about life expanded past my current circumstances. I began thinking about how we are often carried away by traditions that hold no value or purpose.

It was high time we see the harvest of good from our own sacrifices. This would require enough faith to live life fearlessly. Only faith would unlock heaven's innovative ideas and wealth for us to receive the dignity and honor available through Christ Jesus. God made every widow a unique promise to help them at all times, and I was holding on to them.

In the meantime, the verdict for disobeying tradition had been handed down and was to be carried out as follows: I was to surrender my children, house, documents, and properties to my in-laws. Furthermore, I had one month to choose one of my husband's two remaining step-brothers to be my husband; until I decided Moses' body would remain in the mortuary.

"God, punish the devil," I screamed! "This law is not found in my Bible! A woman should not have to choose who to marry while her husband is still lying in the mortuary! What a wicked world. Who could make such a decision?"

I decided to reject fear and shatter their expectations by telling them, "NO!" I refused to be controlled, therefore reconditioned my mind to remain focused on becoming independent! I am worthy of love, joy, and happiness. "Arise, oh my God!"

I stood my ground and told them my husband never asked me to do any of these things! The elders were all silent, except one. He asked me, "What did our son ask you to do?"

I responded, "Moses asked me to make sure that he was buried on the land he purchased with his own money, and I should live with his children and stay in his house."

The elders asked me if that is what I was planning to do, and I said yes. Two days later, I received a call from my late husband's uncle, a Christian Elder in the Assembly of God Church. He said,

"Omowumi, if all you said to the elders yesterday was what Moses asked you to do and you are ready to do so, go ahead. But if not, do not."

I thanked him, and Moses Akahome Yesufu was buried July 5, 2011, in Lagos, Nigeria, on the land he purchased. God is good, no matter the raging war! I am so thankful to the Almighty God for victory over my adversary. I know now that a widow who depends on God for wisdom, grace, and strength prevails.

The Point of Making Decisions

The decisions you make as a widow determine your future and that of your children. Every wrong decision brings trouble to the next generation. I decided to help my children build on the legacy of their father instead of their grandmother. Therefore, the course of history has been changed, and a new pattern formed to accomplish the Word of God. We now live in peace. *"That affliction shall not occur the second time." The Bible says in the book of Isaiah 65:21:*

"I will build a house, I will dwell in it. I will eat the fruit of my labour."

Note: When making decisions, you must pray and allow God to lead you. I remember when seven men of God from different locations called to tell me where Moses should be buried. They even had reasons and Bible verses to support their points. Afterward, I prayed and fasted, and the will of God stood with my decision to bury my husband in Lagos.

The Seven Years of Denial

By this time, I had done everything my late husband instructed me to do and experienced much success. However, in the process, I completely forgot about myself. My life had become about protecting my children, properties, and remaining in the Word of God. There was no lack in my life, yet I was lost in grief and wouldn't allow anyone to console me. I could not remember the woman I was before I got married. My heart was sealed up. Then God reminded me that *"I am wonderfully and fearfully made"* to fulfill His good purpose on earth.

Widows, awake, and remember you are human; you are not a spirit. We must find our way back into the plans of God.

Experiencing Guilt in Widowhood

Some Widows will experience intense feelings of shame and sadness because they somehow think they are responsible for their husbands' death. There is also the feeling of having committed an offense against the dead, whether real or imagined.

In the early stages of widowhood, I suffered from guilt. I felt as if I was the blame for all that happened to my husband. Doubts had me second-guessing my decision about informing Moses' family when he first became ill. Other widows may lament how they could've prevented accidents by keeping their husbands home or getting them to the hospital on time. I've even heard women say that they nagged their husband so much, he wanted to die!

Just stop that because it's all lies of the devil! None of it will turn back time- It was his time to die.

Carrying such strong feelings of shame and sadness have caused anxiety, mental and physical illness, and sometimes, premature death. I often didn't eat well, linking it to my husband's lack of appetite during his illness. I vicariously kept Moses alive by mimicking his behavior, thinking, if he were alive, he would do it this way, so let me do it that way as well. I monitored my behavior by speaking a certain way or keeping quiet. I felt that I shouldn't wear my beautiful clothes but remain shrouded in grief.

All of that was a load of crap! Where were all of these things written in the Bible? The answer is nowhere because they are all self-imposed!

It is time to arise and shake off the beast. You are capable of doing great things if you allow God to work through you. God knows you all by name, brother and sister, Widows and Widowers. To help alleviate these feelings, please consider meditating on the scripture Romans 12:1-2.

"I appeal to you therefore, brothers, by the mercies of God, to present your bodies as a living sacrifice, holy and acceptable to God, which is your spiritual worship. Do not be conformed to this word, but be transformed by the renewal of your mind, that by testing you may discern what is the will of God."

Here are five steps to help you move forward:

1. Live your life
2. Be authentic
3. Beautify yourself
4. Live orderly
5. Develop and Expand

Fix Yourself in The Plan of Life

Many African widows forget that they exist, and that God has given them a purpose and plan. Therefore, their desire to live grows dim.

I am encouraging you to find your purpose, explore your goals, and live your dreams! You are an all-powerful Widow Warrior with the infinite wisdom of the ages! You deserve to experience joy! It is imperative that you laugh, play, and happily serve God.

Detach yourself from negative energy by creating a relaxing moment for yourself. Visit the beach and splash in the water. Go out with friends and eat good food. Spoil yourself a little. I say to you in love; it was your husband that died, not you, so live your life in a good and Godly way.

Today, I am resilient, strong, generous, and compassionate. But my greatest accomplishment of all is helping to heal the widow community.

Daily Affirm

I am strong. I am resilient. I am enough. I am Brave. I am bold. I am confident. I am smart. I am kind. I am beautiful. I am radiant. I am unique. I am wonderfully made. I am free. I am in control. I am valued. I am loved. I am special. I am equal. I am important. I am full of life. I am human.

Christian Widows and Widowers Empowered Initiatives in Nigeria.

Currently, I have been recognized as a woman of faith and given opportunities to mentor and advocate for Widows and Widowers in Nigeria. I also serve as a Life Coach to empower and motivate individuals seeking to expand their horizons.

I know my Moses would be proud of me. He had a heart for the lost, and my heart was toward the broken. Together our story and legacy will bring hope.

In Conclusion

During my journey, I moved from denial to reality in accepting that my Moses was gone to be with the Lord, and we would meet later in eternity. I no longer grieve like I have lost; I grieve like a conqueror. What was meant to crush me has finally made me strong.

Furthermore, I have discovered, in my widowhood journey, that I am resilient- A victor, not a victim, an encourager not a despiser. I now believe that it's possible to love after loss- That's right, I discovered that I can love again.

By the grace of God, I can boldly say, my life is good; I am blessed! The greatest lesson is, do not be moved by the opinions of others, but be moved by the Word of God which says, *"I am wonderfully and beautifully made."* Hallelujah!

About Beatrice Omowumi Yesufu

Beatrice Omowumi Yesufu is the founder of the highly esteemed Christian widows and widowers empowered initiative Nigeria, a non-profit organization caring for widows and widowers mentally, emotionally, socially, economically and spiritually. Beatrice Yesufu is a pastor in one of RCCG parish in Nigeria. She also manages her late husband organization call Mayob Properties. She was recognized by LOANI Egypt, Hall of Fame Florida USA, she is also an award winner by Global Trade Chamber USA, 100 successful Women in Business USA.

Connect with Beatrice Yesufu at yesufubeatrice@gmail.com

AFTERWORD

In that day shall there be a great mourning in Jerusalem, as the mourning of Hadadrimmon in the valley of Megiddo.
-Zechariah 12:11

Although "*A Widow's Resilience*" was written from a woman's perspective, the very essence of losing a spouse is just as heartfelt - if not more so - from a man's point of view. I am a widower. My wife, Annie, transitioned to be with the Lord, after nearly 34 years of marriage. Upon her death, those days after, were the longest, darkest, saddest days of my life. I was distraught. I was lost. I was alone. I asked the Lord to deliver me from the valley of Megiddo- the valley of sorrow. I took a leave of absence from work and filled my days with staying away from my home - the home in which Ann and I had shared our entire marriage. Down deep, I knew, however, that I had to trust God, gird up my strength in Him, and move forward.

One day, a few months later, the Lord answered my prayer. In walked a beautiful woman, whom the Lord spoke to my heart - "This is who I have for you." I was in disbelief but I trusted God. That beautiful woman, LaTanya Orr, the curator of this project, became my wife just a few months later. Our whirlwind romance is still being told. We are testaments of God's faithfulness and unfailing love toward us. He knew our destinies - from before the foundations of the world - would suddenly collide without any warning. Do we understand it? Does it make sense to our human minds? No, not at all. The Lord works in mysterious ways and His wonders never cease. Our vows to our blessed spouses - to love, honor, and cherish, ended at "til death do us part". No guilt, no shame, no condemnation. A new season of life to love was and is in front of LaTanya and I. It is my hope that the wisdom keys and the love stories shared in this book, shine as a beacon of hope for your new season. There is for certain, with God's leading, life and love after death do us part.

-Melvin D. Richard

About Melvin D. Richard

Melvin D. Richard is an evangelist and senior respiratory therapist, whose 30-year bi-vocational career allows him to minister to those who are physically, as well as spiritually, hurting. Richard preaches the Gospel of the Lord Jesus Christ locally and internationally. He is the published author of, *"The Boxing Match: Conscience vs. Crime -The Role of Evangelical Protestant Christianity in Crime Prevention".*

Connect with Melvin Richard at melvinrichard28@gmail.com

About the Curator

Brand strategist and certified life coach, **LaTanya Orr,** strategically equips entrepreneurs, corporate executives, and ministry leaders with award-winning concepts that showcase their brand brilliance with intention and maximum impact. Her sought-after expertise in marketing communications and graphic design spans more than two decades. Known as the Creative Crusader, LaTanya assists her clients in personal discovery — to wield their power, purpose, and influence to reveal their extraordinary.

LaTanya is a published writer and author of the book, "*Strike A Pose: 7 Red Carpet Strategies Every Entrepr-eneurial Woman Must Have to Position Her Brand with Style and on Purpose.*" She is the producer and curator of, *"A Widow's Resilience: Wisdom Keys for Moving Forward in Life and Love After Death Do Us Part,"* anthology project.

Connect with LaTanya at concierge@latanyaorr.com

About the Editor

Chicago native **Dr. Monica Handy** is a content editor, play-wright, author, and the sole proprietor of COOTW Entertainment and Literary Works. Her accomplishments in the literary arena include, but are not limited to:

- COOTW Literary Works E Magazine"- Spotlighting Christian talent and stories of human interests.
- The Stage play, "You Reap What You Sow" (adapted from the novel "Battered Clergy from Victim to Victor" by Dr. Joseph B. Howard)
- The Stage play, "Taking Back My Yes" -Short play giving voice and platform to victims/minors of sexual abuse.
- She penned six novels and co-created "Collaboration in Motion."
- Created and edited content for authors, playwrights, and various creative works.

In 2014, Monica was awarded an Honorary Doctorate for her contributions to the Christian community in Sacred literature. Additionally, in 2018 she was licensed in the Office of Evangelism. Books by M. Handy are available in various Chicago and suburban Library locations. Copies are also available in Minneapolis' (Hennepin County) Public Libraries. Dr. Monica Handy has four grown children, three grandchildren, two daughters-in-law, one temperamental pooch, and a never-ending partnership with God.

Connect with Monica Handy at enteringthepromise@gmail.com

NOTES